Government at a Glance: How Hungary Compares

This work is published under the responsibility of the Secretary-General of the OECD. The opinions expressed and arguments employed herein do not necessarily reflect the official views of OECD member countries.

This document and any map included herein are without prejudice to the status of or sovereignty over any territory, to the delimitation of international frontiers and boundaries and to the name of any territory, city or area.

Please cite this publication as:
OECD (2015), *Government at a Glance: How Hungary Compares*, OECD Publishing, Paris.
http://dx.doi.org/10.1787/9789264233720-en

ISBN 978-92-64-23352-2 (print)
ISBN 978-92-64-23372-0 (PDF)

The statistical data for Israel are supplied by and under the responsibility of the relevant Israeli authorities. The use of such data by the OECD is without prejudice to the status of the Golan Heights, East Jerusalem and Israeli settlements in the West Bank under the terms of international law.

Photo credits: Cover © Vinicius Tupinamba/Shutterstock.com.

Corrigenda to OECD publications may be found on line at: *www.oecd.org/about/publishing/corrigenda.htm*.

Foreword

In the aftermath of the global financial crisis, the Hungarian government has started an ambitious public sector reform programme with the aim of modernising its public administration and improving service delivery to its citizens and businesses. Tight budget constraints, combined with low trust in government and in public institutions more generally, have made these reforms all the more urgent and necessary, but at the same time very challenging. While the Hungarian government succeeded in reducing its budgetary deficit, leading to its removal from the excessive deficit procedure of the European Union in 2013, the public administration in Hungary, like in many other OECD countries, is striving to meet the legitimate expectations of its citizenry for greater access, responsiveness and quality of public services and to ensure that public money is well spent.

The OECD-Hungary Strategic Partnership for Public Administration Reform, which started in 2012, aims to provide the Hungarian government with adequate support in the design and implementation of public sector reforms through cross-country learning and by looking at emerging good practices. As part of this Partnership, this first country-focused edition of *Government at a Glance: How Hungary Compares* presents recent comparable data on key indicators of government activities and performance in Hungary, compared with its neighbouring countries (Austria, Czech Republic, Germany, Poland, Slovak Republic and Slovenia) as well as the OECD average.

The main goal of this publication is to identify progress and persisting challenges in public sector reform in Hungary and to highlight areas where public sector efficiency might be further improved in future years. It provides indicators on a wide range of government activities, including public finance management, public employment and pay, administrative burden for businesses, and the delivery of services in two key areas (health care and education).

The different chapters in this publication reflect discussions with the Hungarian government on the main priority areas for reform where Hungary might be able to learn good practices from neighbouring and other OECD countries, as well as areas where Hungary may be leading the way.

This publication is a companion to *OECD Public Governance Reviews: Hungary* (forthcoming) which, at the request of the Hungarian government, will go deeper into providing a set of more tailored and specific recommendations on how to best implement and monitor progress of public sector reforms in Hungary.

Acknowledgements

The production of *Government at a Glance: How Hungary Compares* would not have been possible without the contribution of the Hungarian government, which financed the project and provided assistance to the OECD Secretariat in gaining access to data and to other information, and commented on the draft. The OECD also acknowledges the contribution of other international organisations, especially Eurostat, the International Labour Organization and the World Bank for sharing some of the data presented here.

This publication was drafted by Guillaume Lafortune under the supervision of Zsuzsanna Lonti (Senior Project Manager) and Edwin Lau (Head of Division), and under the direction of Rolf Alter (Head of the Public Governance and Territorial Development Directorate). Major comments and contributions were received from Luiz De Mello, Alessandro Lupi (Chapter 1 on public finances), Barbara Ubaldi (Chapter 4 on e-government), Gaetan Lafortune (Chapter 5 on health care) and Corinne Heckman, Soumaya Maghnouj and Ignacio Marin (Chapter 6 on the education system). We would also like to thank Filippo Cavassinni for reviewing the publication and in guaranteeing consistency with the *OECD Hungarian Public Governance Review* (forthcoming). Valuable comments were also received from Alvaro Pina, responsible for the *OECD Economic Surveys: Hungary 2014*, working in the OECD Economics Department. The document will also be shared with the Government at a Glance Steering Group and with the Public Governance Committee as a floor document.

Kate Lancaster provided editorial support. Julie Harris prepared the manuscript for publication.

Table of contents

Tables

Figures

Figures *(continued)*

Figures *(continued)*

Figures *(continued)*

Figures *(continued)*

Executive summary

This edition of *Government at a Glance: How Hungary Compares* presents recent trends in the Hungarian public administration, at a time when important public sector reforms are taking place. It is a companion to the 2015 *OECD Public Governance Reviews: Hungary*, which will further analyse the consequences of recent public sector and territorial reforms and provide a set of specific recommendations to achieve further progress.

In 2011, the first Program for Public Sector Reform in Hungary was released, followed by an updated version in 2012. Two years later, a Public Administration and Public Services Development Strategy 2014-2020 was launched, which identifies a series of objectives and ways to measure progress to improve public service delivery over the medium term. This *Government at a Glance: How Hungary Compares* focuses on some of the main priority areas for reform, including the reduction of administrative burdens for businesses, higher uptake of e-government services and improved efficiency of health care and education services.

Hungary was hit hard by the economic crisis, with a "double dip" recession in 2009 and 2012. Major efforts to reduce the budgetary deficits that intensified with the arrival of the new administration in 2010 led to the removal of Hungary from the excessive deficit procedure of the European Union in 2013. However, these reforms involved significant cuts to social protection and benefits. Public satisfaction with government services has generally increased in Hungary in recent years, but it remains lower than in many other Central and Eastern European Countries (CEECs) in important areas like health care and education. As in many other OECD countries, an ongoing challenge for the Hungarian government will be to implement a mix of policies to promote economic growth and job creation, while at the same time reducing income inequalities and geographic disparities in access to key public services. The indicators presented in *Government at a Glance: How Hungary Compares* shed light on the progress achieved by Hungary in recent years, as well as priority areas for further improvement in the years ahead.

The Hungarian government remains large and is increasingly centralised

Despite recent cuts in spending, Hungary continues to have a large government sector, with general government revenues and expenditures accounting for nearly 50% of the economy. This share remains significantly higher than in most other CEEC and OECD countries. General government employment represents 18.8% of the total labour force in Hungary, which is higher than in any of its neighbouring countries and the OECD average (15.5%).

The stated objective of the 2010 State Territorial and Administration Reform (STAR) was to achieve efficiency gains in public spending and move towards greater harmonisation in public service delivery across the country through a re-centralisation of public resources.

This ambitious reform led to a significant transfer of jobs from local governments to the central government, notably in the area of health and social services.

Following the economic crisis, a greater share of public spending in Hungary was allocated to promote economic development and job creation while spending on social protection and education have decreased as part of broader austerity measures

In 2012, public expenditure to promote economic development and job creation represented a higher share of government spending in Hungary than in most other CEEC and OECD countries. On the other hand, between 2009 and 2012, social protection expenditures in Hungary decreased, although it remained higher in 2012 than in most other CEEC countries. Public spending on education is relatively low in Hungary and has decreased in the years following the economic crisis. This may have a negative effect on long-term growth prospects.

Use of digital government services has increased, but there is room for further growth

The Hungarian government has put remarkable efforts into promoting e-government as part of its public administration modernisation strategy, but the use of digital government services by citizens and businesses remains limited.

In 2013, only about half of the population interacted with the Hungarian government via online services. This is comparable to the CEEC average, but below the OECD average. As in other countries, the use of e-government services in Hungary still varies significantly by education level (for citizens) and firm size (for businesses).

The Hungarian government has also taken important steps to develop electronic procurement systems in recent years as a means to increase transparency and efficiency in the public procurement process, but the use of these electronic procurement services by businesses still remains limited and below the average in CEEC and other OECD countries.

The Hungarian health system remains too "hospital centric" and there are persistent issues of access to health care for certain population groups

As in many other OECD countries, the health care system in Hungary remains too "hospital centric"; efficiency gains might be achieved by strengthening access to health care outside hospitals.

The Hungarian government has made serious investments since 2010 to improve access to care for the population in the regions, notably through the creation of outpatient units in 20 rural areas.

Still, a relatively high proportion of the population in Hungary in 2013 reported having some unmet needs for medical examination, due to financial reasons, geographic distance to services or for other reasons.

Expenditure on pharmaceuticals are significantly higher than the OECD average with less than half paid publicly, reflecting high out-of pocket medical spending by households compared to most neighbouring and OECD countries.

Further actions may be needed to ensure that all citizens have access to needed care in Hungary, regardless of their ability to pay or where they live.

Hungarian students perform below their peers in neighbouring countries and relatively few obtain a university degree

Hungary spends less than its neighbouring countries on primary and secondary education and the performance of its students on international tests such as the Programme for International Student Assessment (PISA) are also lower.

School location and the socio-economic background of students continue to play a significant role in students' performance in Hungary, more so than in many other OECD countries. The salaries of teachers are also much lower than in most other CEEC and OECD countries, but the recent pay raises they obtained from the government should improve their situation and help attract and retain a greater number of good teachers.

Despite relatively high graduation rates from secondary education, the percentage of young people obtaining a post-secondary (tertiary) degree remains low in Hungary. This might limit the capacity of Hungary to compete and prosper in an increasingly knowledge-based economy.

Reader's guide

Objectives of the publication

The main objective of the *Government at a Glance* series is to provide reliable, internationally comparable data to compare government activities and their results across OECD member countries. Compared to other OECD publications (e.g. Economic Surveys, Country Reviews) the main objective **is not** to provide detailed analysis and tailored policy advice and recommendations, but to provide a dashboard set of indicators on public sector activities and performance. Three editions of *Government at a Glance* have been released (2009, 2011 and 2013) as well as one regional edition focussing on Latin American and Caribbean countries (2014). This publication is the first attempt by the OECD Secretariat to apply the *Government at a Glance* methodology, while focussing on one particular country and comparing it to selected and relevant neighbouring countries, as well as to the OECD average. Since 2011, the Swedish Agency for Public Management produces its own Swedish "Government at a Glance", re-using the data from the original OECD publication, called *The Swedish Public Administration from an International Perspective.*

Country comparison

In this publication, Hungary is compared only to its neighbouring countries and the OECD average. An average for the four Central and Eastern European countries (CEECs) is calculated for most figures and includes the Czech Republic, Poland, the Slovak Republic and Slovenia. Hungary is also compared to Austria and Germany. Comparing Hungary to countries which are close in terms of geography, history and culture enables more relevant benchmarking, which also takes into consideration the specific context in which CEECs operate.

Period covered

Wherever possible the figures generally provide data for the period before the crisis (2007), during the crisis (2009) and most recent available data (either 2012 or 2013 in most cases). This enables us to analyse the impact of the crisis on different aspects of public administration in Hungary compared with its neighbouring countries. This publication is based on the information available at the time it was completed in October 2014.

Definition of general government

Data on public finances are based on the definition of the "general government" sector found in the System of National Accounts (SNA). Accordingly, general government comprises ministries/departments, agencies, offices and some non-profit institutions at the central, state and local levels, as well as social security funds. Data on revenues and expenditures are presented for both central and sub-central levels of government (which includes only the local level of government in Hungary, while it also includes the regional/state level in other countries, for instance federal countries) and (where applicable) for social security funds. Data on employment generally refer to the broad public sector, including general government and public corporations, such as publicly owned banks, harbours and airports.

Conceptual framework

This *Government at a Glance: How Hungary Compares* edition provides indicators describing government activities and performance. It focusses on the whole "production chain" of government, including inputs, processes and outputs/outcomes in selected areas (Figure 0.1).

Contextual factors

The Introduction, Annex A and Annex B provide some background information on the current economic, social and political situation in Hungary and other Central and Eastern European countries. This is useful to understand public sector reforms that have been undertaken in recent years in Hungary and its neighbouring countries.

Public resources

Chapters 1 and 2 focus on the two main resources (inputs) of governments: public finances and human resources (public employment). Chapter 1 provides recent data from the System of National Accounts (SNA) on the government's revenues and expenditures as well as on the production costs, outsourcing and fiscal decentralisation. Chapter 2 reviews recent trends in general government employment in Hungary, and in compensation of public employees.

Administrative processes

Process indicators refer to a range of public management practices and procedures undertaken by a government to implement its policies. In this publication, the focus is on two broad categories of processes: the level and trends of administrative burden for businesses, and the level and trends of uptake among citizens and businesses of online public services (e-government platforms and systems). Chapter 3 provides data and indicators on the general business environment, the administrative barriers to entrepreneurship, the complexity involved in finding information about government rules and regulations and the administrative burden for start-ups. Chapter 4 on e-government services provides data on the general level of use of online services among citizens and businesses, including the disparities that exist in the use of these services among different population groups and business size. It also describes the uptake of e-procurement systems.

Sectoral outcomes

Finally, Chapters 5 and 6 provide more in-depth analysis on two sectors of importance in the Magyary Program and Public Administration and Public Services Development Strategy 2014-2020: health care and education. For both sectors the structure of the analysis is the same: each section starts with a presentation of the general level of satisfaction among the population and some key outcomes indicators in the sector (e.g. for health, the evolution of life expectancy at birth since 2000; for education, the Programme for International Student Assessment (PISA) results for 15 year-old students). It then analyses the performance of the health and education systems, in terms of access to services, and the efficiency and effectiveness of the delivery of these services.

Conceptual framework

Contextual factors

What is the social , political and economic context in which governments operate?

Introduction

Chapter 0

Public resources

What is the size and structure of government spending? How much revenue does government collect ? What is the size of public sector employment and other inputs?

Public finances	Public sector employment and compensation
(Chapter 1)	**(Chapter 2)**

Administrative processes

How does government work? How do citizens and businesses interact with the government? How do they access and use government services and administrative documents?

Administrative burden	E-Government services
(Chapter 3)	**(Chapter 4)**

Sectoral outcomes

What are some of the main goods and services funded and/or delivered by the government? What is the resulting impact on citizens?

Health care system	Education system
(Chapter 5)	**(Chapter 6)**

Introduction

This introductory chapter provides background material to help the reader better understand the context of current public sector reforms in Hungary. It starts by presenting a series of indicators on the main macroeconomic aggregates (economic growth rate, unemployment rate, debt and deficit levels). It then discusses trust in government levels before and after the crisis, and public satisfaction levels with government services and institutions, as reported in international perception surveys.

The context for public sector reforms to improve access to, and the efficiency of, public services in Hungary

The context for public sector reforms in Hungary is challenging:

- On the economic side, the country has just emerged from a double dip recession in 2009 and 2012.
- Real GDP grew somewhat moderately, by 1.2% in 2013 (above the CEEC average growth rate).
- The unemployment rate remains above 8%.
- Central government debt is among the highest across the OECD (85.2% of GDP in 2012, using the System of National Accounts [SNA] definition).
- Fiscal consolidation programmes introduced by the government in 2010 led to a reduction of public deficits, which was achieved partly through significant one-off items (primarily asset transfers from private pension funds to the state pension fund), expenditure cuts in social protection and family benefits and tougher control of local governments' borrowing transactions.
- Citizen confidence in the national government has increased in recent years, but remains below the OECD average.
- Public satisfaction with government services is generally higher than in neighbouring countries but is lower than the OECD average, especially in the sectors of health and education.
- And finally, the general level of well-being measured by the OECD Better Life Index is lower in Hungary than in all CEEC countries and OECD countries. This is associated with rising inequalities and poverty rates, and persistent geographic gaps in citizen ability to access public services across regions.

Economic growth and unemployment

Hungary was hit relatively hard by the crisis, with a double recession in 2009 and 2012 (Figure 0.1). In 2013, the economy grew by 1.2% in real terms, which is higher than the average among CEEC countries and comparable to the average across the OECD (1.3%). Increases in the levels of investment (+5.9% compared to 2012), government consumption (+1.6% compared to 2012) and domestic demand (+1.6% compared to 2012) were the main drivers of economic growth in Hungary in 2013 (Annex D). According to the *OECD Economic Outlook*, economic growth in Hungary should reach about 2% in 2014 and 2015, close to the OECD average.

The unemployment rate in Hungary grew rapidly during the Great Recession of 2009, from around 8% in 2008 to 11% of total labour force in 2010 (Figure 0.2). The unemployment rate then stabilised at around 11% between 2010 and 2012 before descending to about 10% in 2013. The decline in the unemployment rate is expected to continue in 2014 and 2015 in Hungary although it should remain above the OECD average.

Figure 0.1. **Economic growth in real terms in Hungary has exceeded the regional average growth in 2013, but is expected to remain somewhat modest over the medium term**

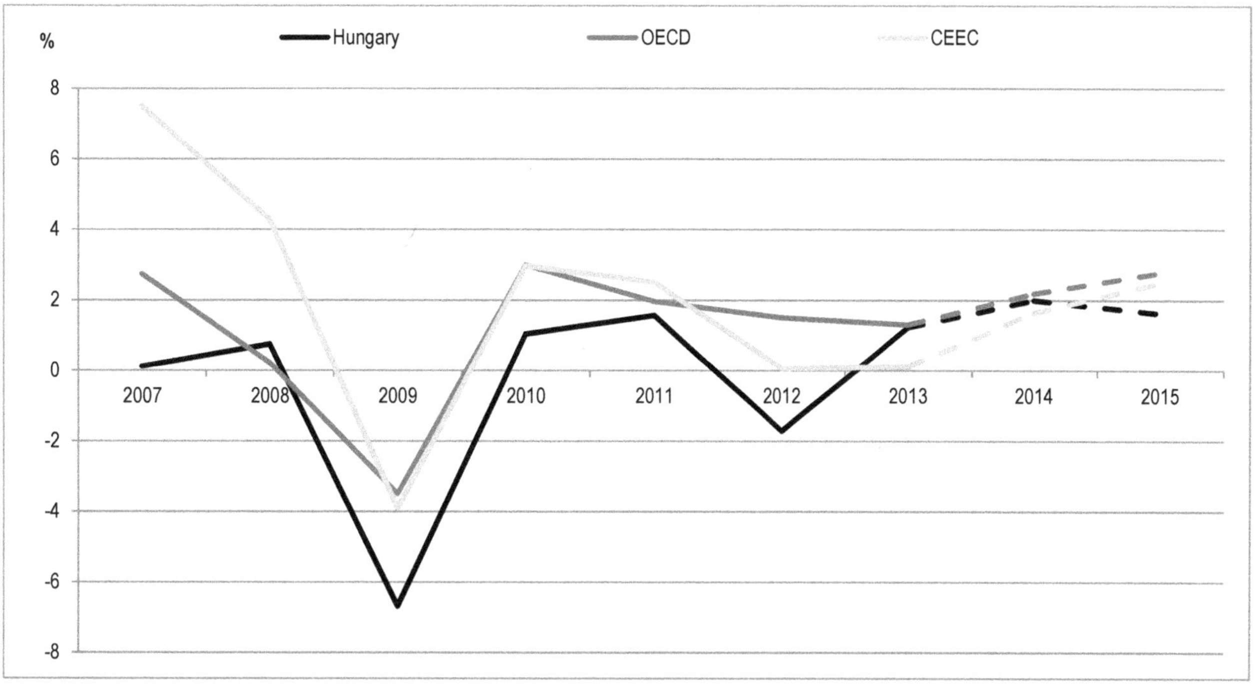

Source: OECD (2014a), "OECD Economic Outlook No. 95", *OECD Economic Outlook: Statistics and Projections* (database), http://dx.doi.org/10.1787/data-00688-en (accessed on 21 March 2015).

StatLink http://dx.doi.org/10.1787/888933203253

Figure 0.2. **Hungary's unemployment rate is higher than before the crisis, but declining**

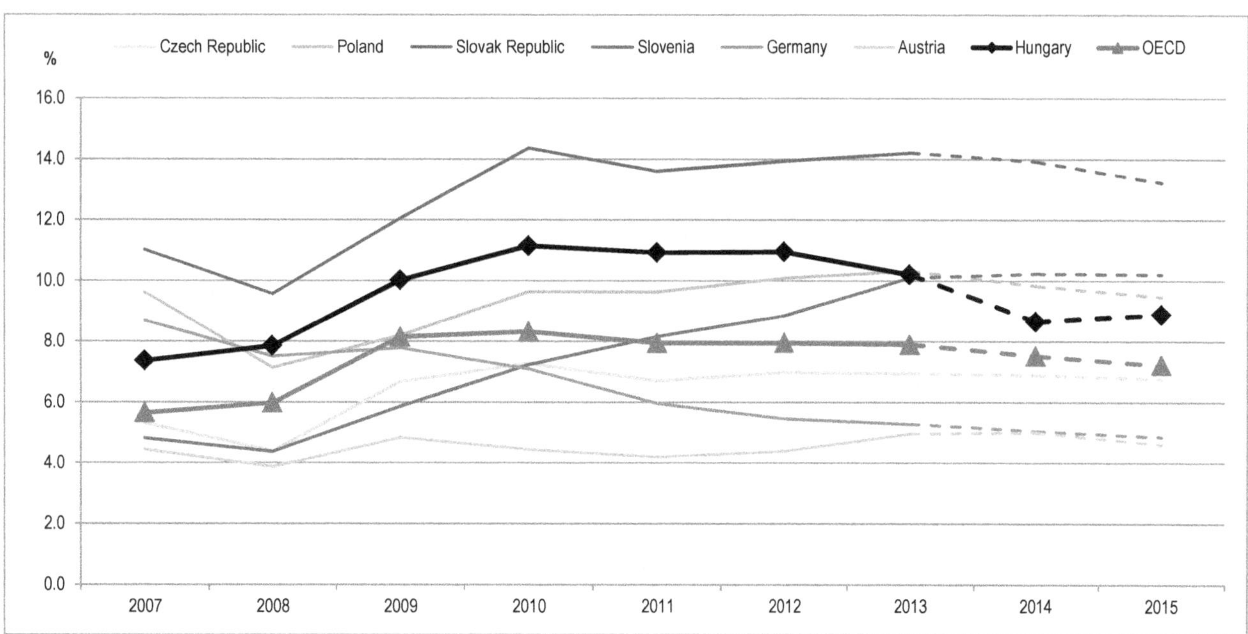

Source: OECD (2014a), "OECD Economic Outlook No. 95", *OECD Economic Outlook: Statistics and Projections* (database), http://dx.doi.org/10.1787/data-00688-en (accessed on 21 March 2015).

StatLink http://dx.doi.org/10.1787/888933203264

Fiscal deficit and debt

The economic crisis has undermined the fiscal position of most OECD countries, increasing further accumulated public debts (Figure 0.3). As a share of the economy, the central government debt[1] in Hungary in 2012 (85.2%) was above all CEEC countries (55.4% on average) and higher than the OECD average (71.6%). Between 2007 and 2012, the central government debt has increased by 15.84 percentage points in Hungary. The new Hungarian government took over most of the debt of municipalities in recent years, which explains the high increase in central government debt and the relative stability of local governments' debt over the period.

Figure 0.3. **Central government debt as a percentage of GDP in Hungary significantly increased during the crisis and is among the highest across the OECD**

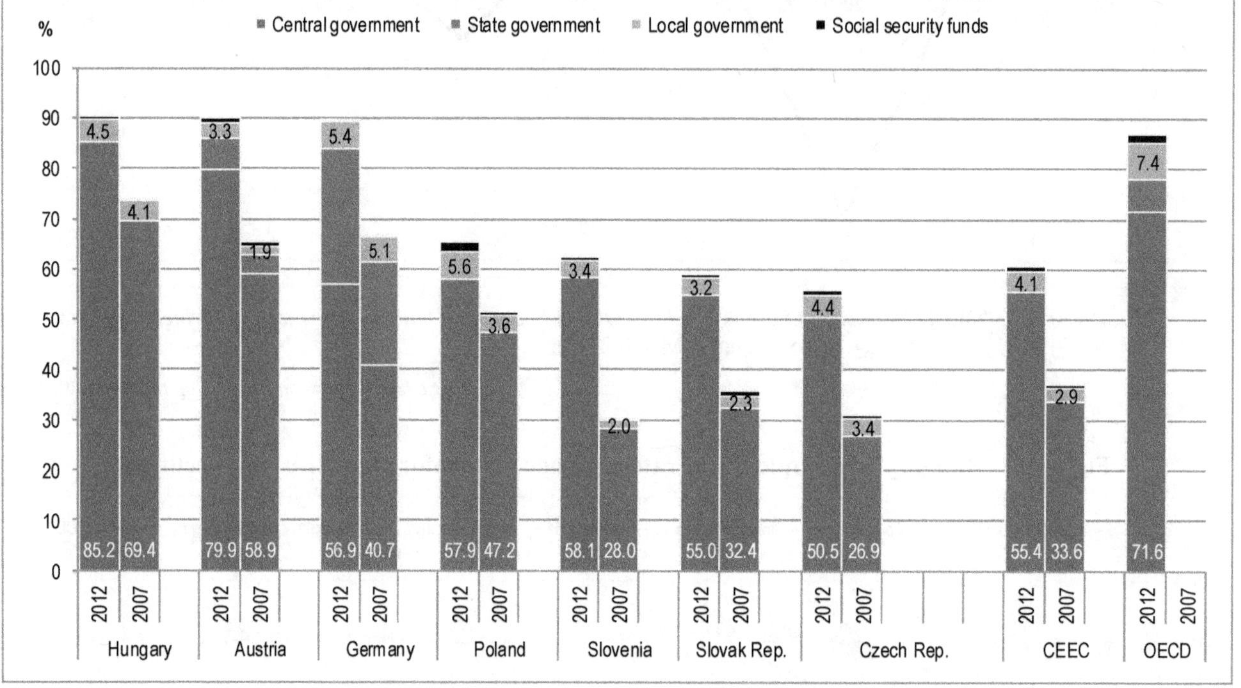

Source: OECD (2014b), *OECD National Accounts Statistics* (database), http://dx.doi.org/10.1787/na-data-en (accessed on 21 March 2015).

StatLink http://dx.doi.org/10.1787/888933203271

The new constitution, adopted in 2011, created a constitutional base for the limitation of local governments' borrowing. The Economic Stability Act adopted the same year contains a general rule stating that borrowing transactions from local governments (or any other transaction with equivalent effect) must be approved *ex ante* by the central government offices. In 2012, the total general government deficit in Hungary represented 2.2% of the GDP (ESA 95) which corresponds to a decrease of 2.4 percentage points compared to 2009 (Figure 0.4). Looking only at the local government fiscal balance, it rose from a 0.4% deficit in 2009 to a 0.5% surplus in 2012.

Figure 0.4. **Hungary's government deficit as a percentage of GDP has significantly decreased in recent years, in part due to the new fiscal rules on the borrowing transactions of municipalities**

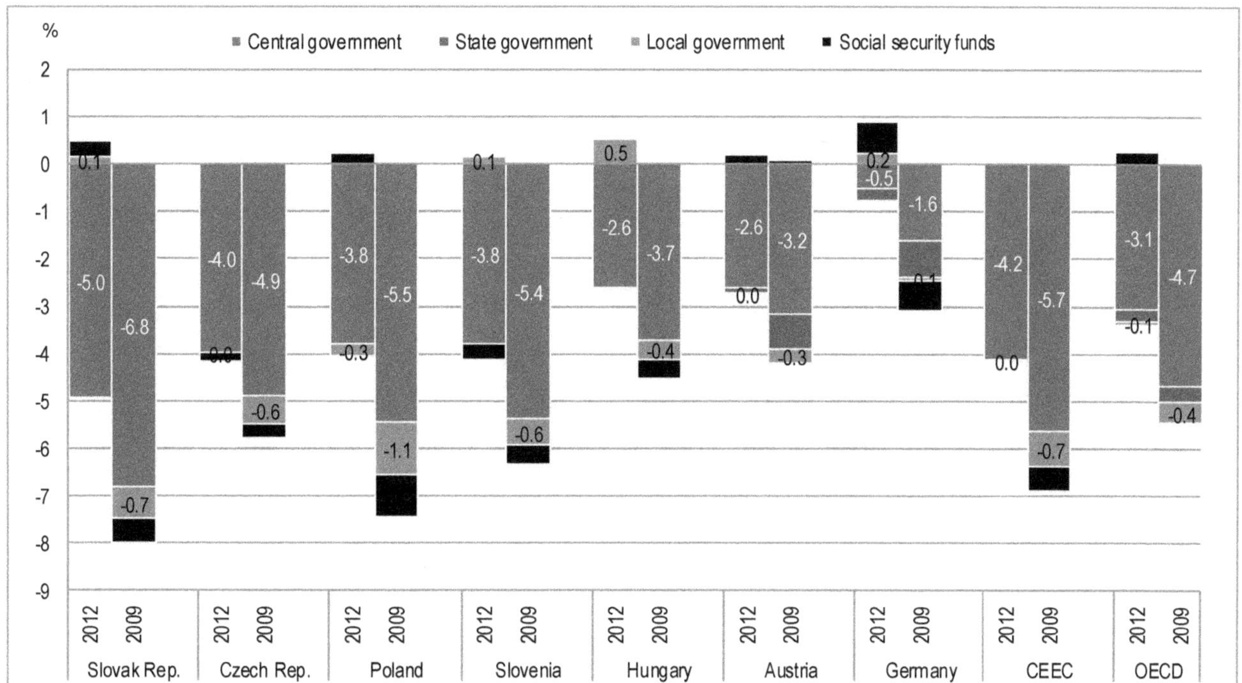

Source: OECD (2014b), *OECD National Accounts Statistics* (database), http://dx.doi.org/10.1787/na-data-en (accessed on 21 March 2015).

StatLink http://dx.doi.org/10.1787/888933203285

As a response to fiscal pressure, the Hungarian government introduced extensive programmes to reduce deficits and debts over the medium term. According to the OECD Survey on Restoring Public Finance (OECD, 2012), the fiscal consolidation plans designed by the Hungarian government between 2010 and 2015 were the most significant of all CEEC country plans, including important expenditure reduction measures (both operational and programme spending cuts) and revenue enhancement measures.

Trust in government and satisfaction with public services

Despite important expenditure reduction measures over past years, public confidence and satisfaction with the government has increased in Hungary since 2007, although it remains low compared to the OECD average. In 2013, about 33% of the Hungarian population reported having confidence in their national government, compared with 25% in 2007 and 20% in 2009. This is higher than the CEEC average (21%), but lower than the OECD average (40%). Trust in national leadership also increased between 2007 and 2013 in Hungary, rising from 19% to 28% in positive public opinion, while it decreased in all other CEEC countries (22% on average in 2013) (Gallup World Poll, 2014). However, cross-country comparisons should be made with caution, as trust in government also depends on cultural factors and can fluctuate rapidly, depending on events.

Figure 0.5. **Public confidence in Hungary's national government has increased in recent years**

% of people who declare having confidence in their national government (2007, 2009 and 2013)

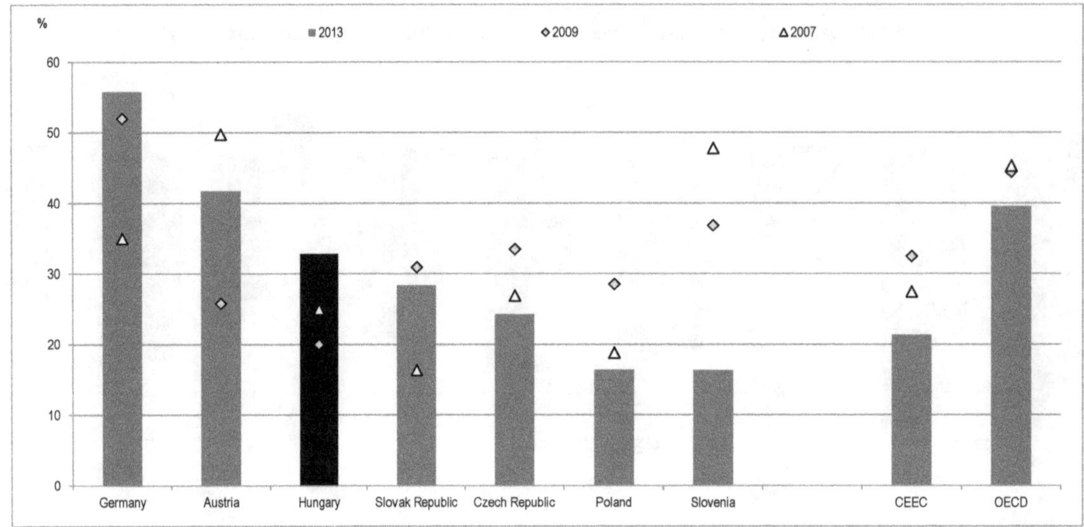

Source: Gallup World Poll, www.gallup.com.

StatLink http://dx.doi.org/10.1787/888933203296

Regarding satisfaction with public services and institutions, the levels of public satisfaction have generally increased since 2007, but remain low by OECD standards (except for satisfaction with public transport, which is slightly higher than the OECD average) (Figure 0.6). Satisfaction with public services is greater in general in Hungary than in other CEEC countries, except for satisfaction with the health care and the education systems, which are slightly lower than the CEEC average.

Figure 0.6. **Hungarian citizens' satisfaction with public services is generally higher than in other Central and Eastern European countries, except in the sectors of health and education**

% of people who declare being satisfied with the availability and quality of public services and institutions (2013)

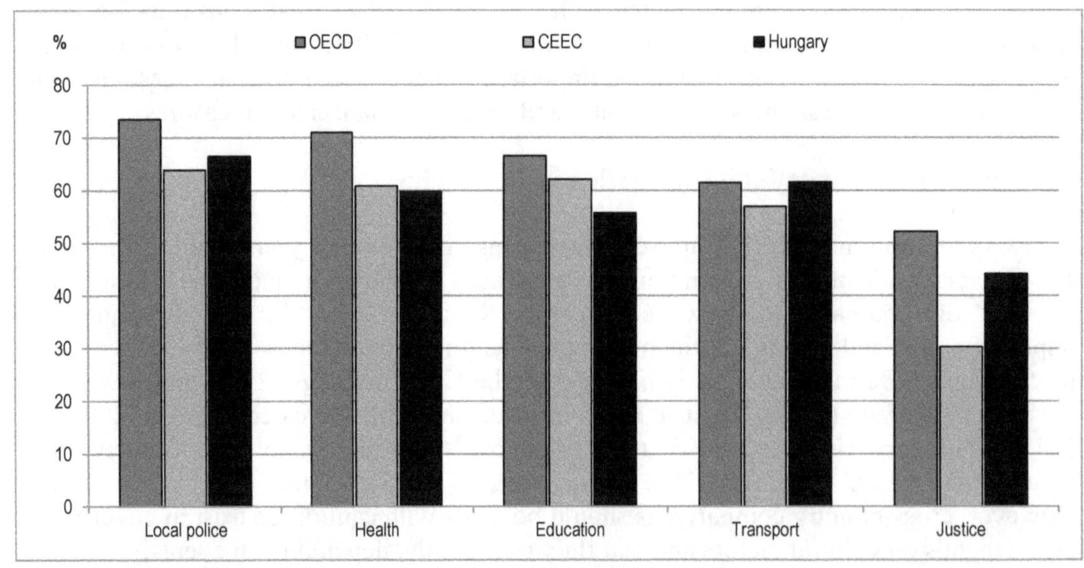

Source: Gallup World Poll, www.gallup.com.

StatLink http://dx.doi.org/10.1787/888933203300

Well-being and inequality

The overall quality of life in Hungary, as measured by the OECD Better life Index, is among the lowest across the OECD and there are increasing issues regarding income inequalities and poverty. In 2013, Hungary ranked low compared to neighbouring countries and OECD countries on most of the components of the OECD Better Life Index (OECD, 2014c).

In recent years, income per capita in Hungary has only moderately increased, and has remained lower than its neighbouring countries and OECD countries. Income inequalities and material deprivation have increased sharply in Hungary, compared to the period before the crisis. After a slight decrease between 2007 and 2010 from 25.6 to 24.1, the GINI coefficient has markedly increased since 2010 in Hungary (28.0 in 2013), and is above the CEEC average (26.0), though still below the EU28 average (30.5 in 2013) (Figure 0.7). The poverty rate after taxes and transfers (percentage of people who live with less than 50% of the median national income) has risen from 6% in 2007 to more than 10% in 2013, which is higher than the CEEC average (9%) (OECD, 2014d). The number of people who report not having enough money to buy food has also increased in Hungary, rising from 17% before the crisis to 31% in 2012, which is more than twice the share in OECD countries (14%) (OECD, 2014d).

Figure 0.7. **The GINI coefficient after taxes and transfers has markedly increased since 2010 in Hungary and was above the CEEC average in 2013**

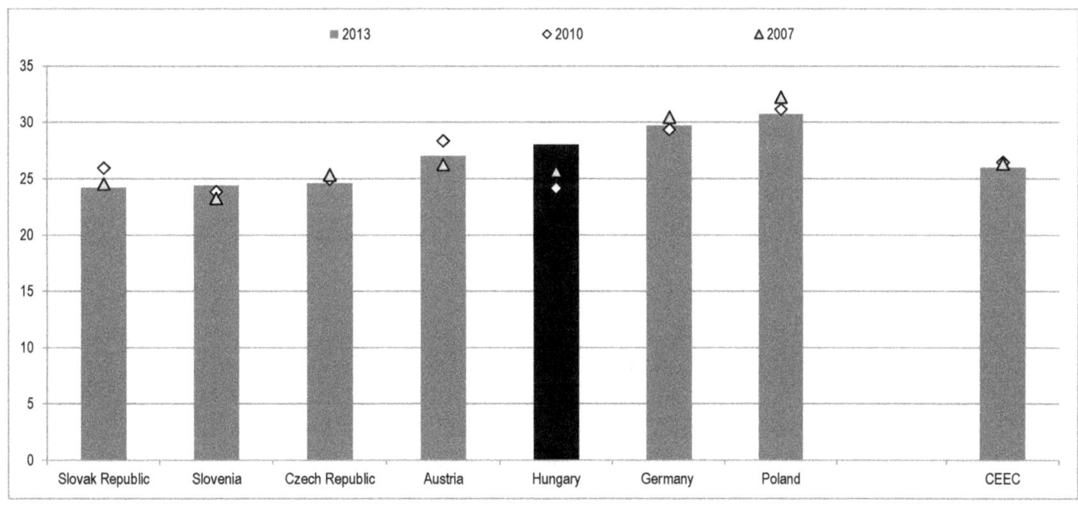

Source: Eurostat (2014), *Survey of Income and Living Conditions (SILC)* (database), http://ec.europa.eu/eurostat/web/microdata/european_union_statistics_on_income_and_living_conditions.

StatLink http://dx.doi.org/10.1787/888933203317

There are also persistent gaps in the access to quality public services between the capital region and other regions in Hungary (Figure 0.8). In the northern great plain region in Hungary, the share of households with broadband access is for instance significantly lower than the national average (measured in the access to public services dimension) while the homicide rate is much higher (measured by the safety dimension). In addition, the average life expectancy is well below the level reached in the capital region and the share of labour force with at least secondary education is also much lower.

Figure 0.8. **There are persistent geographic inequalities in the access to certain public services in Hungary**

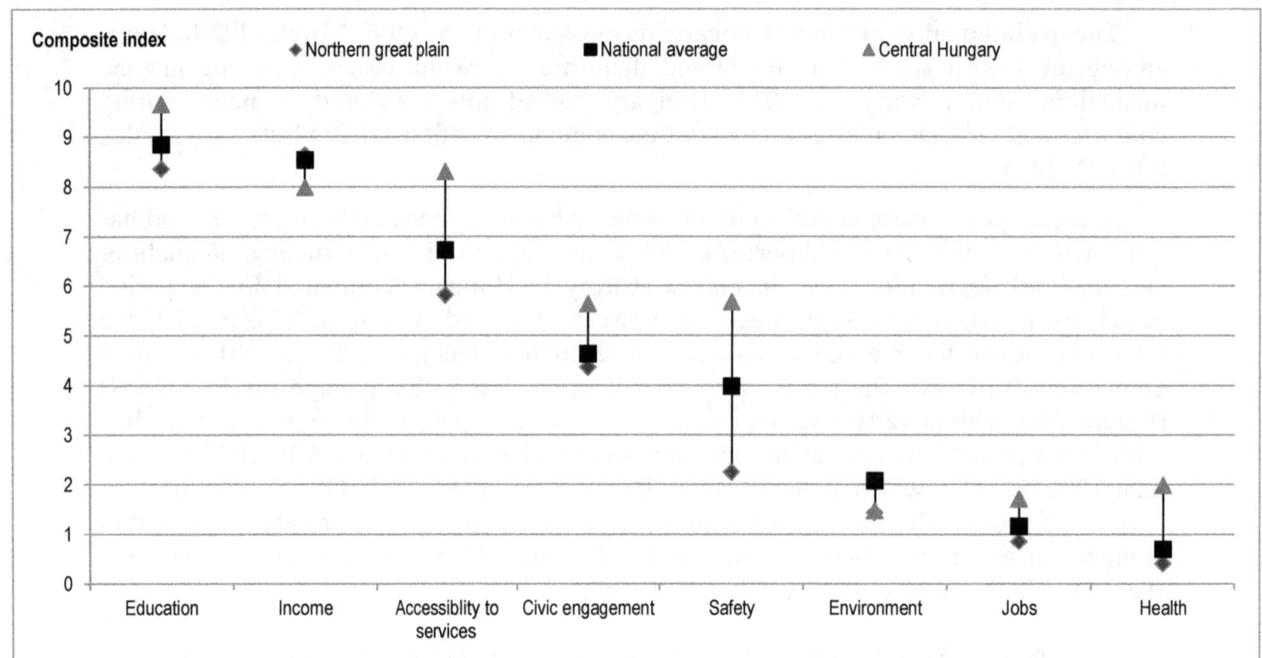

Source: OECD (2014e), OECD Regional Well-Being Index, www.oecdregionalwellbeing.org/.

StatLink http://dx.doi.org/10.1787/888933203324

Notes

1. Data are derived from the *OECD National Accounts Statistics* (database) which are based on the System of National Accounts (SNA), a set of internationally agreed concepts, definitions, classifications and rules for national accounting. The SNA definition of debt differs from the definition applied under the Maastricht Treaty, which is used to assess EU fiscal positions. Firstly, gross debt according to the Maastricht definition excludes not only financial derivatives and shares and other equity, but also insurance technical reserves and other accounts payable. Secondly, debt according to Maastricht definition is valued at nominal prices and not at market prices.

Bibliography

European Commission (2013), “Assessment of the 2013 National Reform Programme and Convergence Programme for Hungary”, Commission Staff Working Document, SWD(2013)367final.

Eurostat (2014), *Survey of Income and Living Conditions (SILC)* (database), http://ec.europa.eu/eurostat/web/microdata/european_union_statistics_on_income_and_living_conditions.

GKI (2012), “An Economic Recovery Plan For Hungary – A Blueprint of the Government’s Actions for the 2014-2018 Period”, GKI Gazdaságkutató Zrt.

OECD (2014a), “OECD Economic Outlook No. 95”, *OECD Economic Outlook: Statistics and Projections* (database), http://dx.doi.org/10.1787/data-00688-en (accessed on 21 March 2015).

OECD (2014b), *OECD National Accounts Statistics* (database), http://dx.doi.org/10.1787/na-data-en (accessed on 21 March 2015).

OECD (2014c), *OECD Economic Surveys: Hungary 2014*, OECD Publishing, Paris, http://dx.doi.org/10.1787/eco_surveys-hun-2014-en.

OECD (2014d), *OECD Social and Welfare Statistics* (database), http://dx.doi.org/10.1787/socwel-data-en (accessed on 21 March 2015).

OECD (2014e), OECD Regional Well-Being Index, www.oecdregionalwellbeing.org/.

OECD (2014f), *Society at a Glance 2014: OECD Social Indicators*, OECD Publishing, Paris, http://dx.doi.org/10.1787/soc_glance-2014-en.

OECD (2013a), *OECD Regions at a Glance 2013*, OECD Publishing, Paris, http://dx.doi.org/10.1787/reg_glance-2013-en.

OECD (2013b), *National Accounts at a Glance 2013*, OECD Publishing, Paris, http://dx.doi.org/10.1787/na_glance-2013-en.

OECD (2012), *Restoring Public Finances, 2012 Update*, OECD Publishing, Paris, http://dx.doi.org/10.1787/9789264179455-en.

International surveys measuring confidence and satisfaction with government, institutions and services: Weblinks

Gallup World Poll: www.gallup.com.

Chapter 1

Public finances in Hungary

This chapter describes and analyses the key indicators in public finances helping to shed light on how the Hungarian government is managing its public finances in comparison with its neighbouring countries. Using the System of National Accounts (SNA), it includes indicators on the size of public revenues and expenditures, government production costs and outsourcing as well as on fiscal decentralisation. In order to offer insights on the evolution during the period before and after the economic crisis, most indicators are presented for 2007 and 2012.

This chapter reviews the size and structure of public finances in Hungary.[1] It describes five main findings:

1. As a share of the economy, the size of the Hungarian public sector is relatively large, both in terms of government revenues and expenditures.
2. The recent economic crisis and tax reforms have modified the structure of public revenues, with a larger share coming from EU structural funds and from consumption taxes. The share of public revenues from income and corporate taxes has significantly decreased.
3. On the expenditure side, the Hungarian government spends a greater percentage than its neighbouring countries as well as OECD countries on supporting economic development through a range of programmes directed at the private sector, while it has significantly reduced public spending on social protection and education in recent years to combat large deficits.
4. Government spending on goods and services (such as hospital equipment, transport material, etc.) is generally high, with little use of outsourcing to raise efficiency in public service delivery.
5. Since 2010, the reorganisation of the territorial structure of government led to a centralisation in taxing and spending capacity with a corresponding reduction in the role of local governments.

Government revenues as a share of the economy

In 2012, general government revenues in Hungary represented 46.6% of GDP, which is higher than the Central and Eastern European countries (CEEC) average (39.2%) and the OECD average (41.8%) (Figure 1.1). Between 2001 and 2012, government revenues as a share of the economy increased in Hungary by 2.9 percentage points while they slightly decreased on average in neighbouring countries, and remained relatively stable across the OECD. Government revenues in 2012 were higher in Hungary compared to before the crisis, which is also the case in most neighbouring countries (except Poland which has been less affected by the economic crisis and has recovered more quickly).

Figure 1.1. **General government revenues as a percentage of GDP, Hungary, neighbouring countries and OECD average, 2001, 2007 and 2012**

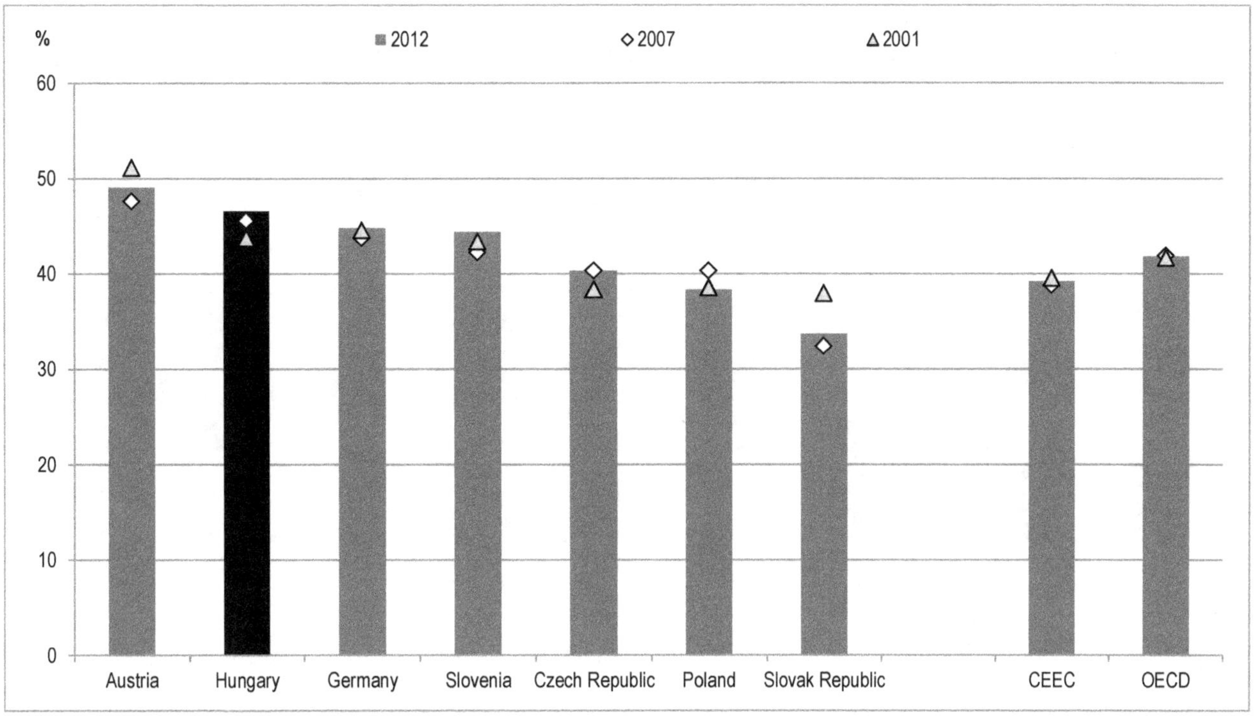

Source: OECD (2014a), *OECD National Accounts Statistics* (database), http://dx.doi.org/10.1787/na-data-en (accessed on 21 March 2015).

StatLink http://dx.doi.org/10.1787/888933202608

Structure and recent trends in government revenues and tax breakdown

Taxes other than social contributions in Hungary represented more than half of all government revenues in 2012 (55.2%) (Figure 1.2). This is more than in all other CEEC countries, but below the OECD average (60.4%). The other half of remaining public revenues in Hungary is composed of social contributions paid by employers and employees (28.6%) and grants and other revenues (mainly grants from EU structural and cohesion funds, but also grants from other international organisations and other revenues derived from sales and fees, property income and subsidies). Compared to the pre-crisis period, the share of taxes and social contributions account for a smaller share of all government revenues, whereas the share of grants and other revenues coming mainly from EU structural funds increased considerably between 2007 and 2012 (+37%).

Figure 1.2. **Structure of general government revenues, Hungary, neighbouring countries and OECD average, 2007 and 2012**

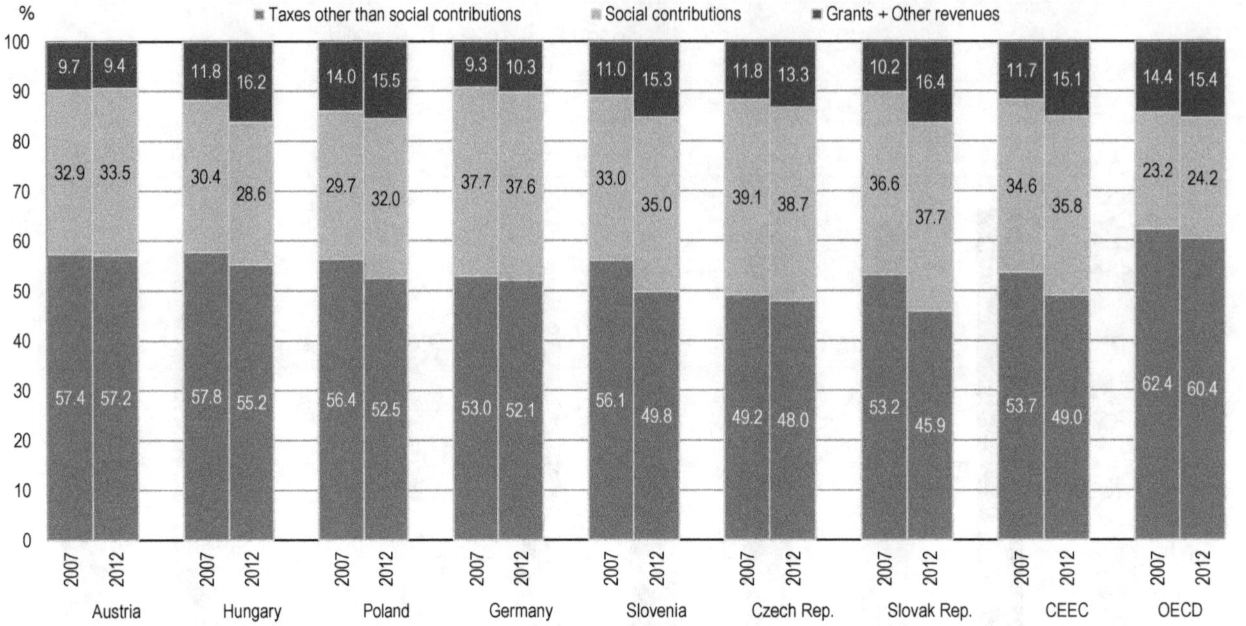

Source: OECD (2014a), *OECD National Accounts Statistics* (database), http://dx.doi.org/10.1787/na-data-en (accessed on 21 March 2015).

StatLink http://dx.doi.org/10.1787/888933202611

There have also been changes in the composition of tax revenues (including social security contributions) in Hungary. In 2009 and 2010, to create a more stable fiscal environment and stimulate economic activities (Johansson, 2008), the Hungarian government introduced a series of tax reforms with the objective to reduce taxes on individual and corporate income and corporate profit and raise taxes on consumption (i.e. goods and services). Compared to the pre-crisis situation, the share of total taxation revenues from consumption taxes increased significantly, rising from 38% in 2007 to 43% in 2011 (the highest share among neighbouring countries), whereas the share of taxes on incomes of households and companies and business profits significantly decreased (-34.5%) (Figure 1.3).

The growing share of revenues from consumption taxes has been achieved mainly by a steady increase of the standard rate of the value added tax (VAT), which rose from 20% in 2008 to 25% in 2009 and up again to 27% in 2012 (the highest rate across the EU), combined with efforts to raise compliance. There have also been some special taxes introduced in certain non-tradeable sectors in recent years that have contributed to fiscal consolidation. The regressive nature of these taxes was reduced by replacing direct taxes with some indirect taxes in 2013 that were designed to be progressive. The proliferation of special taxes amended successively in recent years has also caused, to some extent, instability and uncertainty in the tax and regulatory environment in Hungary (OECD, 2014b). Other fiscal measures include the introduction of a flat tax regime on personal income and the reduction of corporate income taxation (European Commission, 2011).

Finally, in order to offset the increase of the tax wedge in a more targeted way, so as to eliminate tax avoidance that was widespread under the former progressive personal income tax system in the case of certain disadvantaged socio-economic groups, the government introduced in 2013 tax allowances in employers' social security contributions for certain categories of low-income workers.

Figure 1.3. **Breakdown of tax revenues as a percentage of total taxation, Hungary and neighbouring countries, 2007 and 2011**

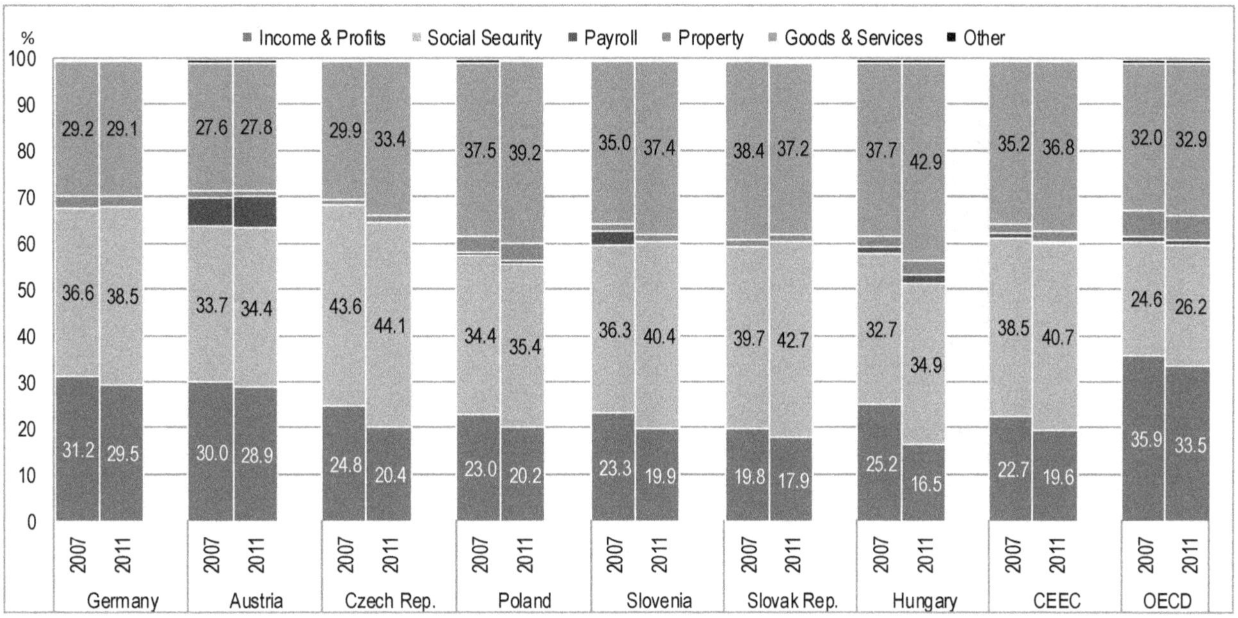

Source: OECD (2013a), *Revenue Statistics 2013*, OECD Publishing, Paris, http://dx.doi.org/10.1787/rev_stats-2013-en-fr.

StatLink http://dx.doi.org/10.1787/888933202621

Government expenditure as a share of the economy

In 2012, general government expenditures in Hungary represented 48.7% of GDP, which is higher than the CEEC average (43.3%) and the OECD average (45.1%) (Figure 1.4). However, as a share of the economy, public spending in Hungary is now lower compared to pre-crisis levels (-2.0 percentage points) while it has increased in all neighbouring countries and most OECD countries on average over the same period. This is due mainly to significant budget cuts introduced by the Hungarian government since 2010 to reduce large deficits. A large part of these budget cuts have targeted social protection and education.

Figure 1.4. **General government expenditures as a percentage of GDP, Hungary, neighbouring countries and OECD average, 2001, 2007 and 2012**

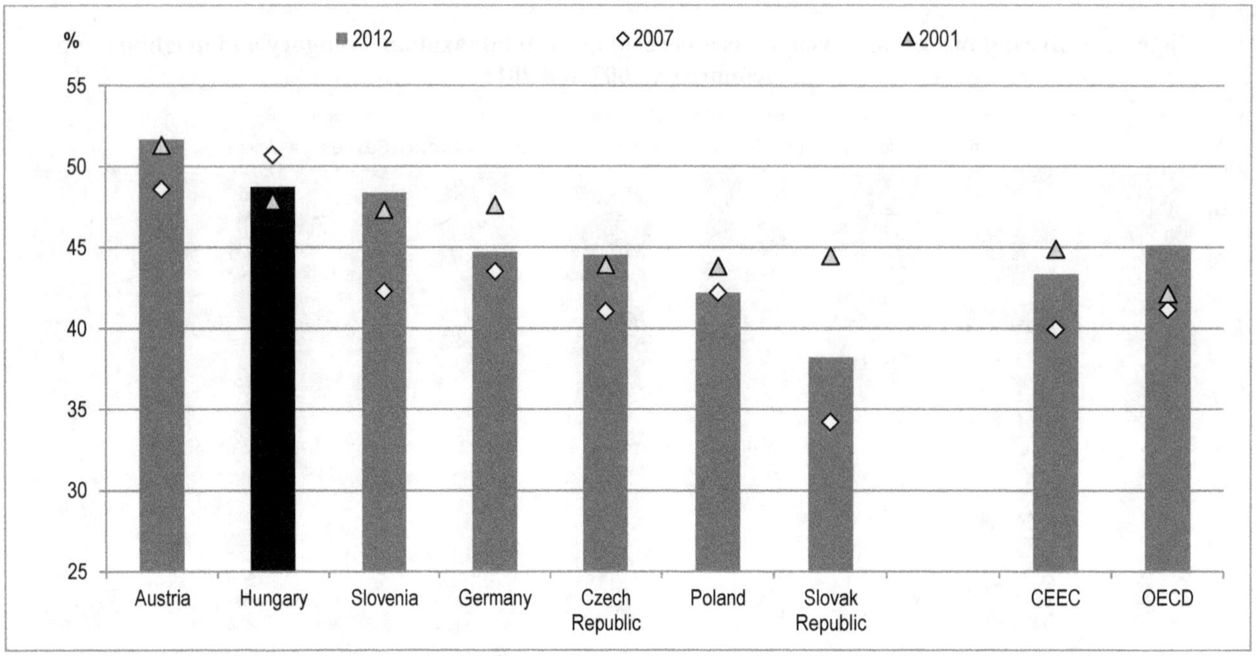

Source: OECD (2014a), *OECD National Accounts Statistics* (database), http://dx.doi.org/10.1787/na-data-en (accessed on 21 March 2015).

StatLink http://dx.doi.org/10.1787/888933202634

Following the economic crisis, social protection expenditure (including pensions, sick pay, child care, family allowances and unemployment benefits) in Hungary decreased significantly in real terms (OECD, 2014c) and as a share of total government expenditure (Figure 1.5). Reforms of the social security and social protection programmes led to an overall decrease of 1.1 percentage points between the levels of social protection spending in 2009 and in 2012, with significant cuts to pension benefits and child and family allowances. This contrasts with the situation in most neighbouring and OECD countries where social protection spending increased as a share of total public expenditure in the years following the economic crisis. For example, neighbouring countries like the Slovak Republic (+2.5 percentage points), Slovenia (+2.2 percentage points) and Poland (+1.2 percentage points) increased their spending on social protection as a share of total public spending due to rising unemployment and government reforms. Social protection expenditure in Hungary in percentage of GDP remains however higher on average than in other CEEC countries (SNA, ESA 95) and family tax allowances were introduced in recent years to mitigate the impact of reduced social protection expenditure.

Figure 1.5. **Evolution of social protection expenditure between 2009 and 2012 (as a share of total public expenditure), Hungary, neighbouring countries and OECD countries**

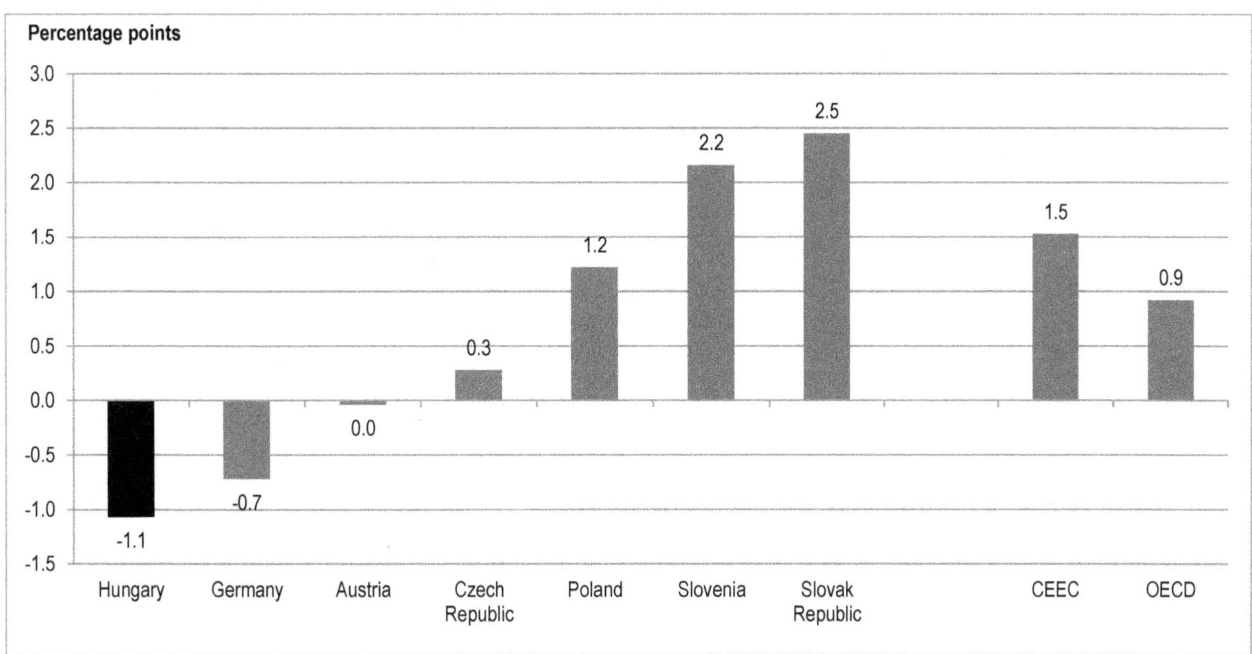

Source: OECD (2014a), *OECD National Accounts Statistics* (database), http://dx.doi.org/10.1787/na-data-en (accessed on 21 March 2015).

StatLink http://dx.doi.org/10.1787/888933202640

Regarding other categories of government expenditure, between 2009 and 2012, the share allocated to education as a share of total public expenditures in Hungary decreased by 0.5 percentage points, now accounting for less than 10% of total spending, which is less than the share of public expenditure dedicated to education in most neighbouring countries and the OECD average (12.3%). The share of health expenditures (10.8%) increased between 2009 and 2012 (+1.0 percentage point), but the share of health spending in total government expenditures remains well below CEEC countries (14.8%) and the OECD average (14.6%).

Structure and recent trends in government expenditure

In 2012 the main public spending categories in Hungary, as in many neighbouring countries and OECD countries, were social protection, general public services (which includes debt services) economic affairs, health and education (Table 1.1). However, in 2012, the structure of government spending in Hungary compared with neighbouring countries and OECD countries varied in at least two important ways: 1) a greater share of public spending is allocated to promote economic development in the private sector; 2) a lower share is allocated to education and health expenditure (see Chapters 5 and 6 for a more detailed description of public spending and performance of the health and education systems in Hungary).

Table 1.1. **Structure of general government expenditures by function, as a share of total general government expenditure (%) in Central and Eastern European countries, 2012**

	General public services	Defence	Public order and safety	Economic affairs	Environmental protection	Housing and community amenities	Health	Recreation, culture and religion	Education	Social protection
Austria	13.0	1.3	2.9	11.3	1.0	1.2	15.4	1.9	10.8	41.3
Czech Republic	11.3	2.0	4.1	12.5	3.1	1.6	17.6	6.1	10.9	31.0
Germany	13.7	2.4	3.5	7.7	1.3	1.0	15.7	1.7	9.7	43.3
Hungary	18.6	1.7	4.0	**12.8**	1.5	1.9	**10.8**	3.9	**9.9**	35.1
Poland	14.1	2.8	4.1	11.0	1.3	2.0	10.9	2.8	12.9	38.1
Slovak Republic	15.9	2.8	6.4	9.3	2.5	2.0	16.3	2.6	10.2	32.0
Slovenia	12.1	2.2	3.7	8.1	1.5	1.6	14.5	3.7	13.3	39.3
CEEC	13.3	2.5	4.6	**10.2**	2.1	1.8	**14.8**	3.8	**11.8**	35.1
OECD	14.0	3.5	3.9	**9.9**	1.7	1.6	**14.6**	2.7	**12.3**	35.9

Source: OECD (2014a), *OECD National Accounts Statistics* (database), http://dx.doi.org/10.1787/na-data-en (accessed on 21 March 2015).

StatLink http://dx.doi.org/10.1787/888933202658

In 2012, public expenditure to promote economic development represented 12.8% of total government expenditure in Hungary, which is higher than the CEEC average (10.2%) and the OECD average (9.9%), but comparable to the Czech Republic. Like in all neighbouring countries, expenditure in the transport sector represented the biggest share of government spending to support economic growth (56.1%) (Figure 1.6).

Compared to its neighbouring countries, expenditure on general economic, commercial and labour affairs was, however, much higher in Hungary (29.4% of total economic affairs expenditure), while it accounted for less than one-fifth of economic affairs spending in CEEC countries on average (18.7%). This category of spending in Hungary includes mainly capital transfers and subsidies to support job creation, and to promote general economic and commercial policies and programmes, including, for instance, the public works programme, which has scaled up since 2009[2] (Figure 1.7).

Figure 1.6. **Structure of government expenditures on economic affairs (as a share of total economic affairs expenditure), Hungary and neighbouring countries, 2012**

General economic, commercial and labour affairs
Agriculture, forestry, fishing and hunting
Fuel and energy
Mining, manufacturing and construction
Transport
Communication
Other industries
R&D Economic affairs
Economic affairs n.e.c.
%
100
85
70
55
40
25
10
-5
39.2
22.6
66.4
8.5
45.1
23.3
56.1
29.4
76.4
6.8
43.0
19.7
55.4
20.6
54.5
18.7
Austria
Czech Republic
Germany
Hungary
Poland
Slovak Republic
Slovenia
CEEC

Note: Data for the Slovak Republic is from 2011 instead of 2012.

Source: OECD (2014a), *OECD National Accounts Statistics* (database), http://dx.doi.org/10.1787/na-data-en (accessed on 21 March 2015).

StatLink http://dx.doi.org/10.1787/888933202667

Figure 1.7. **Government expenditures in general economic, commercial and labour affairs by economic transaction, Hungary and neighbouring countries, 2012**

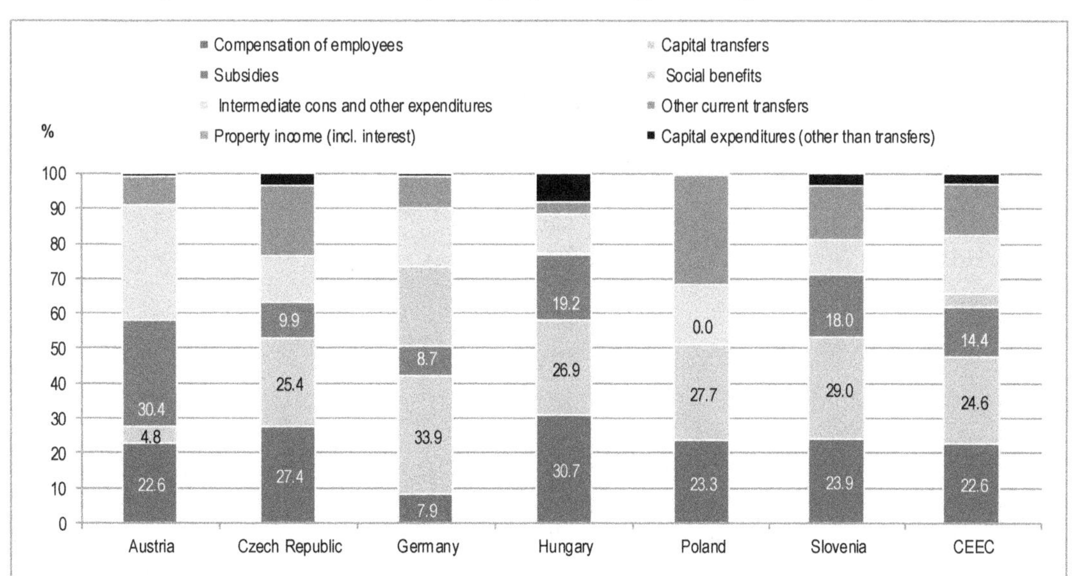

Note: Data for the Slovak Republic is from 2011 instead of 2012.

Source: OECD (2014a), *OECD National Accounts Statistics* (database), http://dx.doi.org/10.1787/na-data-en (accessed on 21 March 2015).

StatLink http://dx.doi.org/10.1787/888933202670

Government production costs

In 2012, the government production costs (the share of government expenditures dedicated to the production of goods and services) represented 23.2% of GDP in Hungary, which is higher than in most neighbouring countries (except Slovenia) and the OECD average (22.8%) (Figure 1.8). Between 2007 and 2012, as a share of the economy, the share of government production costs in Hungary decreased by 1.3 percentage points, while they increased in all other neighbouring countries (except Poland). This has been achieved mainly by a reduction in the compensation package for general government employees (see Chapter 2 on public sector employment). Compared to most other CEEC countries, the government spends relatively more to purchase intermediate goods and services (e.g. to buy material and equipment to provide transportation or health services) and on the consumption of fixed capital (depreciation). The relatively high ratio of the costs of goods and services in Hungary can be explained at least partly by a higher VAT ratio. In 2012 the standard VAT ratio was 20% in the Czech Republic, Slovakia and Slovenia and 23% in Poland, while it reached 27% in Hungary.

Figure 1.8. **Government production costs as a percentage of GDP, Hungary, neighbouring countries and OECD average, 2007 and 2012**

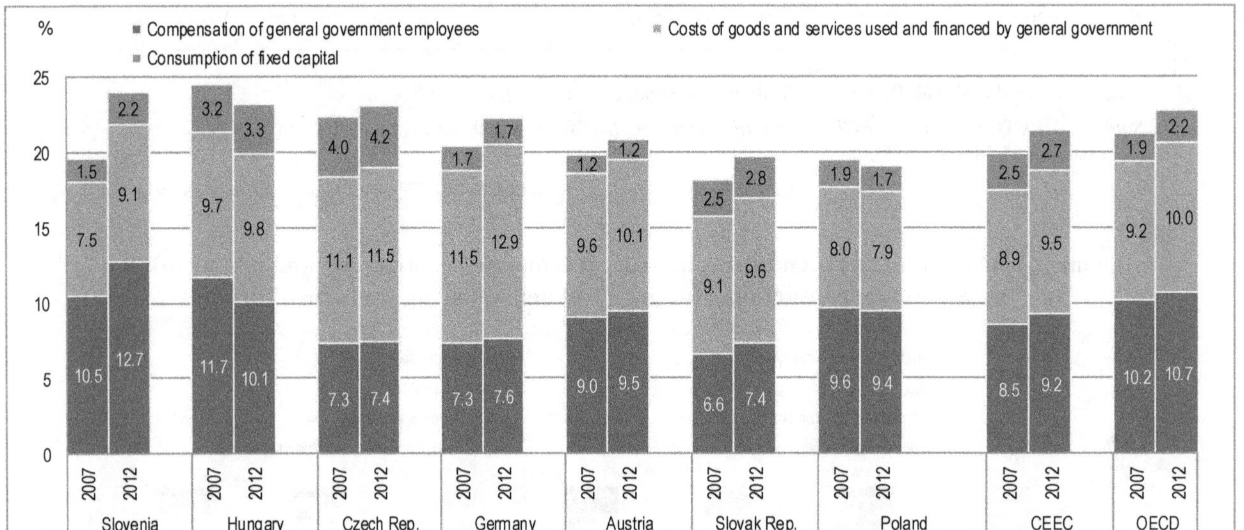

Source: OECD (2014a), *OECD National Accounts Statistics* (database), http://dx.doi.org/10.1787/na-data-en (accessed on 21 March 2015).

StatLink http://dx.doi.org/10.1787/888933202686

Government use of outsourcing

While some governments produce most goods and services themselves, others outsource a large proportion of the production to private companies or non-profit organisations. There are two ways by which outsourcing can take place: governments can either purchase goods and services to be used as inputs in the delivery of final goods and services or they can pay a non-profit or private organisation to provide these goods and services directly to end users (goods and services financed by government, i.e. social transfers in kind via market producers) (OECD, 2013b).

Overall, outsourcing expenditures in Hungary (9.8% of GDP) is comparable both to CEEC countries and the OECD average (10%) and has slightly increased since 2007 (Figure 1.9). However, the share of the production of public goods and services outsourced to a third party to directly provide the service to end users is small (2.3% of GDP) compared to neighbouring countries and OECD average (3.4%). This share has decreased since 2007 while it has increased in all other neighbouring countries and on average across the OECD.

Figure 1.9. **Expenditures on general government outsourcing as a percentage of GDP, Hungary, neighbouring countries and OECD average, 2012**

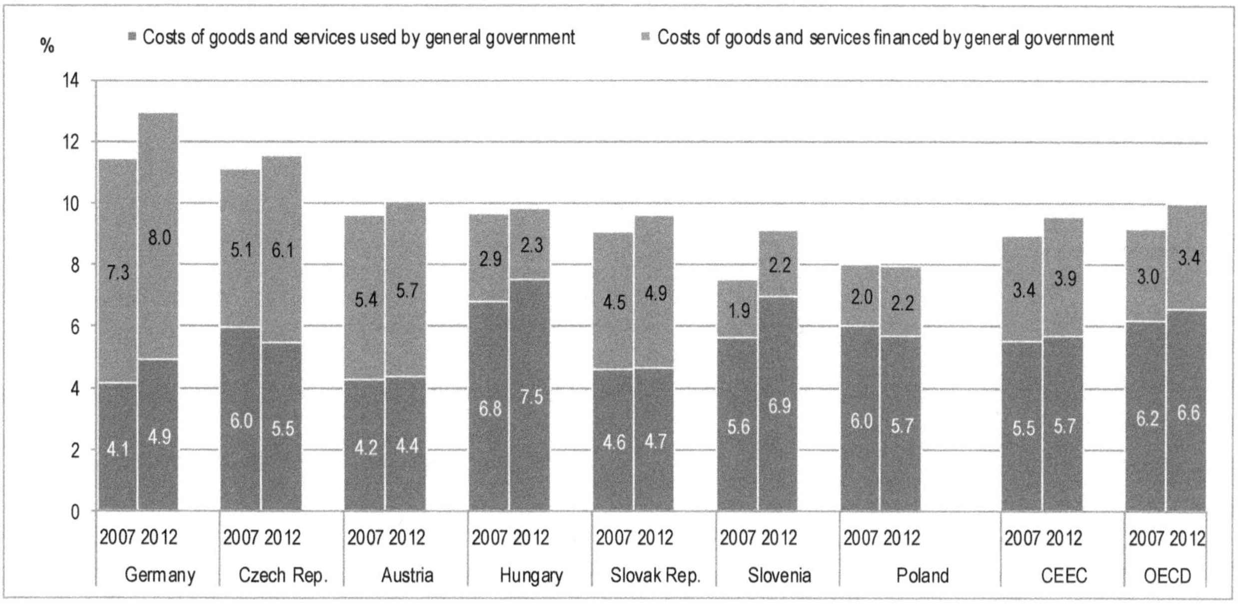

Source: OECD (2014a), *OECD National Accounts Statistics* (database), http://dx.doi.org/10.1787/na-data-en (accessed on 21 March 2015).

StatLink http://dx.doi.org/10.1787/888933202699

Fiscal decentralisation

The territorial reforms introduced in Hungary in the past few years sharply reduced the financial autonomy of municipalities. In 2012, as a share of total government revenues, the sub-central level of government (which includes local level of government in Hungary) collected only 10% of the public revenues in Hungary, which is lower than in all neighbouring countries and half the OECD average (21.7%) (Figure 1.10). Regarding public expenditures, local governments in Hungary spent 18.7% of all public spending, which is also lower than in most neighbouring countries (except the Slovak Republic) and the OECD average (30.2%).

Figure 1.10. **Fiscal decentralisation, Hungary, neighbouring countries and the OECD average, 2012**

%

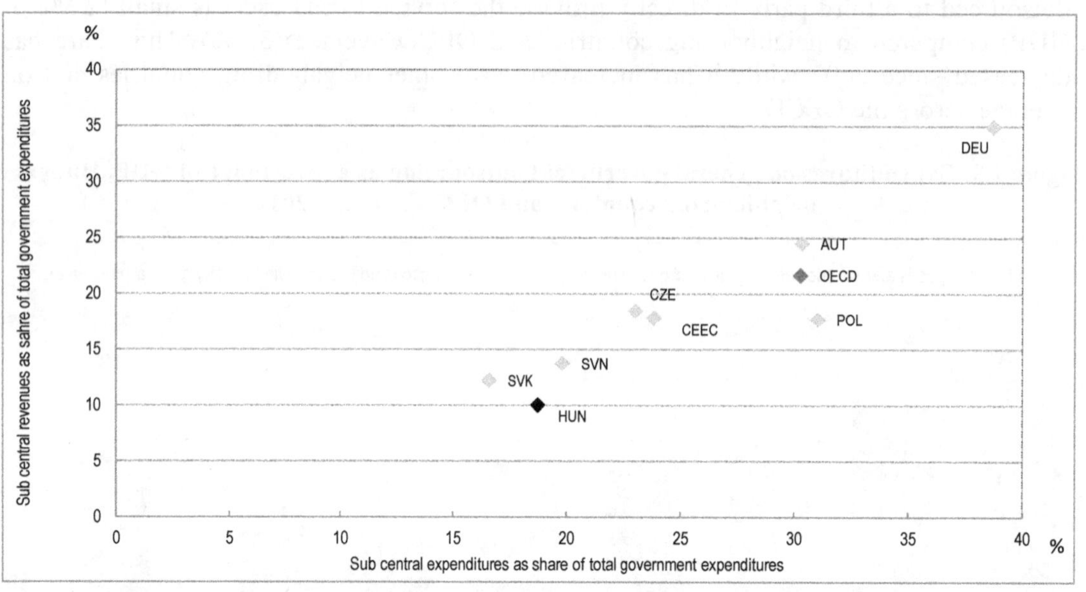

OECD (2014a), *OECD National Accounts Statistics* (database), http://dx.doi.org/10.1787/na-data-en (accessed on 21 March 2015).

StatLink http://dx.doi.org/10.1787/888933202709

Between 2007 and 2012, the share of revenues collected by local government in Hungary decreased by 3.9 percentage points, while it increased in most neighbouring countries and across the OECD on average (+0.3 percentage points) (Figure 1.11). The majority of the municipalities' revenues in Hungary come from transfers from the central government, with local taxes representing less than one quarter of their total revenues (OECD, 2013c).

Regarding government expenditures, between 2007 and 2012, the share of public spending by local governments in Hungary also decreased (-4.5 percentage points) which has also been the case in many of the OECD countries, but to a lesser degree (-1.2 percentage points) (Figure 1.12). Looking more specifically at investment spending, only 37.8% of total public investment was realised by local governments in Hungary in 2012, which is lower than the CEEC average (53.8%) and the OECD average (over 48.3%) (Figure 1.13).

Figure 1.11. **Distribution of general government revenues across levels of government, Hungary, neighbouring countries and OECD average, 2007 and 2012**

OECD (2014a), *OECD National Accounts Statistics* (database), http://dx.doi.org/10.1787/na-data-en (accessed on 21 March 2015).

StatLink http://dx.doi.org/10.1787/888933202716

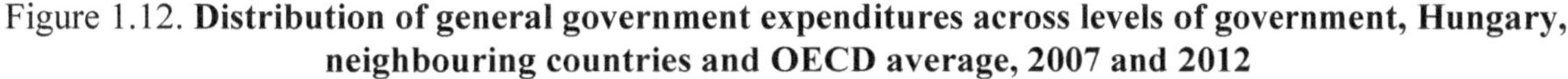

Figure 1.12. **Distribution of general government expenditures across levels of government, Hungary, neighbouring countries and OECD average, 2007 and 2012**

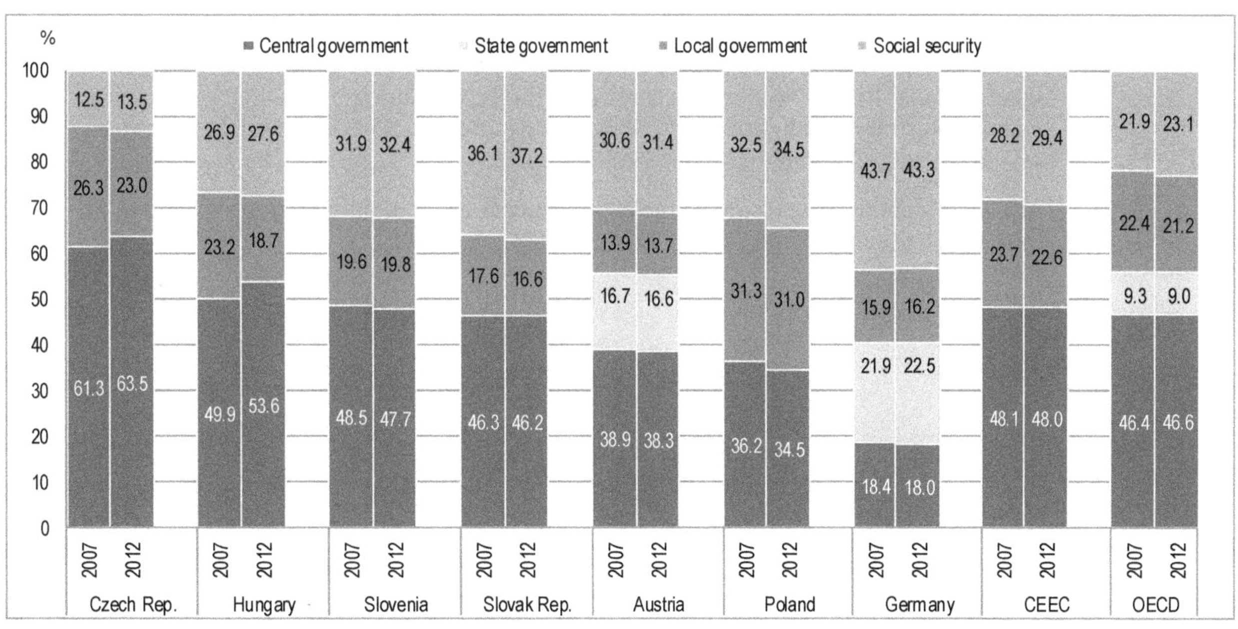

OECD (2014a), *OECD National Accounts Statistics* (database), http://dx.doi.org/10.1787/na-data-en (accessed on 21 March 2015).

StatLink http://dx.doi.org/10.1787/888933202722

Figure 1.13. **Subnational government investments as a percentage of total public investments, Hungary, neighbouring countries and OECD average, 2012**

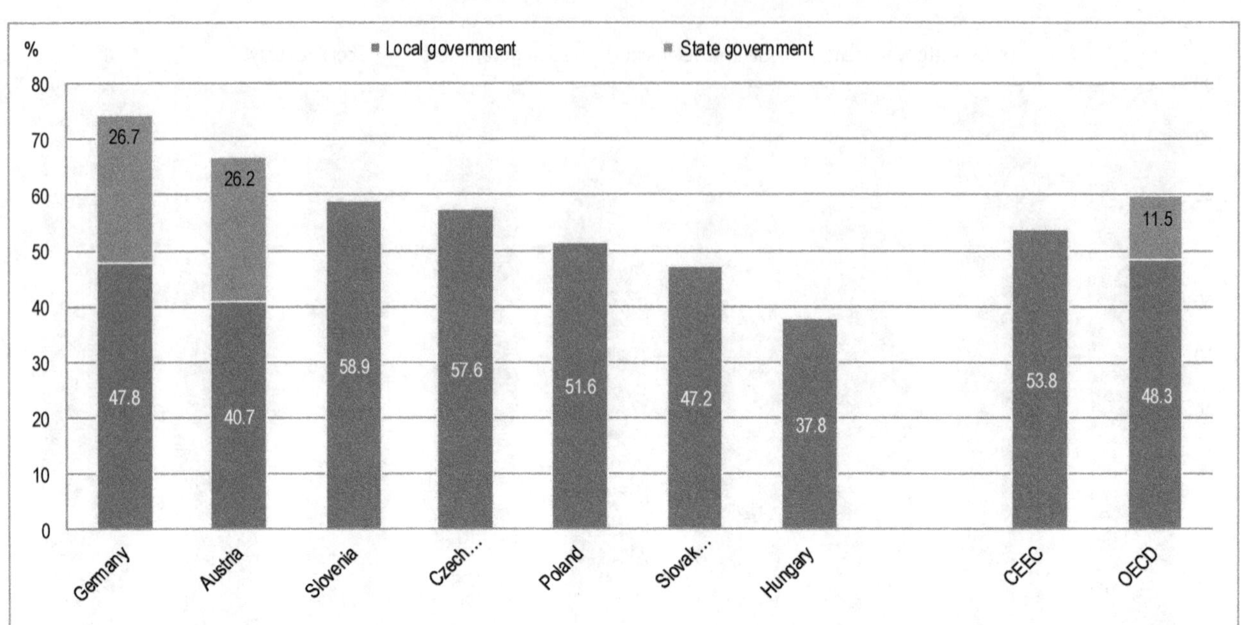

OECD (2014a), *OECD National Accounts Statistics* (database), http://dx.doi.org/10.1787/na-data-en (accessed on 21 March 2015).

StatLink http://dx.doi.org/10.1787/888933202734

Notes

1. This chapter provides public finance data based on the ESA95 SNA methodology. The OECD Secretariat acknowledges that a new SNA methodology was adopted in September 2014 (ESA10) but the transition for expenditures by COFOG were only available starting in January 2015. This is why the OECD Secretariat has kept the previous methodology in this chapter of the report.
2. For a more detailed discussion of the achievements of the public work programmes in Hungary, please refer to OECD, 2014b, pp. 86-87.

Bibliography

Budapest Institute (2013), *Targeting and Impact Evaluation of EU-Funded Active Labour Market Programmes*, Budapest Institute for Policy Analysis, Budapest.

Cournède, B., et al. (2013), "Choosing Fiscal Consolidation Instruments Compatible with Growth and Equity", *OECD Economic Policy Papers*, No. 7, OECD Publishing, Paris, http://dx.doi.org/10.1787/5k43nxq6dzd4-en.

European Commission (2011), "Tax Reforms in EU Member States: Tax Policy Challenges for Economic Growth and Fiscal Sustainability", Working Paper No. 28, Brussels.

Johansson, Å., et al. (2008), "Taxation and Economic Growth", *OECD Economics Department Working Papers*, No. 620, OECD Publishing, Paris, http://dx.doi.org/10.1787/241216205486.

OECD (2014a), *OECD National Accounts Statistics* (database), http://dx.doi.org/10.1787/na-data-en (accessed on 21 March 2015).

OECD (2014b), *OECD Economic Surveys: Hungary 2014*, OECD Publishing, Paris, http://dx.doi.org/10.1787/eco_surveys-hun-2014-en.

OECD (2014c), "Social Expenditure", *OECD Social Expenditure Statistics* (database), http://dx.doi.org/10.1787/els-socx-data-en (accessed on 21 March 2015).

OECD (2014d), "OECD Economic Outlook No. 95", *OECD Economic Outlook: Statistics and Projections* (database), http://dx.doi.org/10.1787/data-00688-en (accessed on 21 March 2015).

OECD (2013a), *Revenue Statistics 2013*, OECD Publishing, Paris, http://dx.doi.org/10.1787/rev_stats-2013-en-fr.

OECD (2013b), *National Accounts at a Glance 2013*, OECD Publishing, Paris, http://dx.doi.org/10.1787/na_glance-2013-en.

OECD (2013c), *OECD Regions at a Glance 2013*, OECD Publishing, Paris, http://dx.doi.org/10.1787/reg_glance-2013-en.

Chapter 2

Public sector employment and compensation in Hungary

This chapter provides a set of indicators on the trends in public sector employment and compensation in Hungary before and after the economic crisis. It provides indicators on the size of general government employment as a share of total labour force and in absolute terms, on the level and evolution since 2007 of compensation of general government employees as a share of total public expenditure, as well as on the distribution of general government employment by levels of government.

This chapter reviews the size and distribution of public sector employment across levels of government in Hungary, together with the developments in compensation costs. It describes three main findings:

1. The size of government employment has slightly decreased as a share of the labour force in recent years in Hungary, but remains among the largest across the OECD.
2. The share of public spending allocated to employee compensation has decreased significantly in recent years, due both to a reduction in staff numbers and in a reduction in salaries and benefits, in response to strong budget pressures.
3. Employment in the central government has been growing at a very fast pace, while the number of people employed by local governments has significantly decreased, especially in the areas of health and social protection.

Size of general government employment and public corporations

In 2011 (the latest year for which data is available for most countries), employment in general government (including all levels of government and social security funds) represented 18.8% of the total labour force in Hungary, which is higher than in any of its neighbouring countries and the OECD average (15.5%) (Figure 2.1). However, compared to 2001, the share of government employment has decreased slightly; part of this reduction is due to the fact that general government employment no longer includes the personnel from the Ministries of Foreign Affairs and Defence in Hungary.

Focussing on the trends over the past five years in Hungary, government employment as a share of labour force reached its peak in 2010 (19.6%) before declining progressively in 2011 and 2012 (Figure 2.2). In absolute terms, government employment fell in 2011, but increased slightly in Hungary in 2012 (+1.4%), albeit at a slower pace than in the rest of the economy, thus explaining the continued reduction in the share.

Contrasting with the share of government employment, the share of employment in public corporations in Hungary (such as post offices, railways, etc.) is much smaller than the Central and Eastern European country (CEEC) average (10.3%) and very similar to the percentage in OECD countries (4.7%) (Figure 2.3). Some CEEC countries such as the Czech Republic and Poland had, for instance, more people employed in public corporations than in the general government in 2011.

Figure 2.1. **Employment in general government as a percentage of the total labour force, Hungary, neighbouring countries and OECD average, 2001 and 2011**

%
■ 2011 ◇ 2001
Hungary, Slovenia, Slovak Republic, Czech Republic, Austria, Germany, Poland, CEEC, OECD

Note: Data for Germany are for 2010. Data for Hungary in 2011 exclude the personnel employed by the Ministry of Foreign Affairs and Ministry of Defence.

Source: ILO (2014a), *ILOSTAT* (database), www.ilo.org/ilostat; OECD (2014a), "Labour Force Statistics", *OECD Employment and Labour Market Statistics* (database), http://dx.doi.org/10.1787/lfs-lfs-data-en (accessed on 21 March 2015). Data for Hungary were provided by the National Statistical Office of Hungary.

StatLink http://dx.doi.org/10.1787/888933202744

Figure 2.2. **Recent trends in general government employment in Hungary, 2007-12**

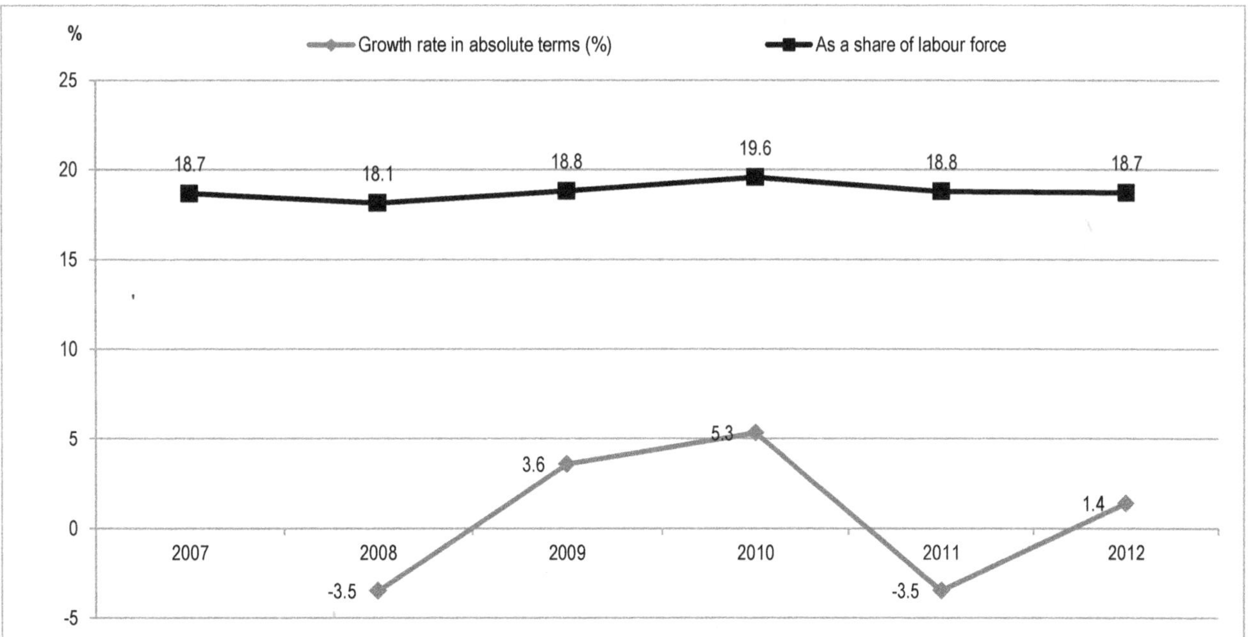

Source: ILO (2014a), *ILOSTAT* (database), www.ilo.org/ilostat. Data for Hungary were provided by the National Statistical Office of Hungary.

StatLink http://dx.doi.org/10.1787/888933202756

Figure 2.3. **Employment in general government and public corporations as a percentage of the labour force, Hungary, neighbouring countries and the OECD average, 2011**

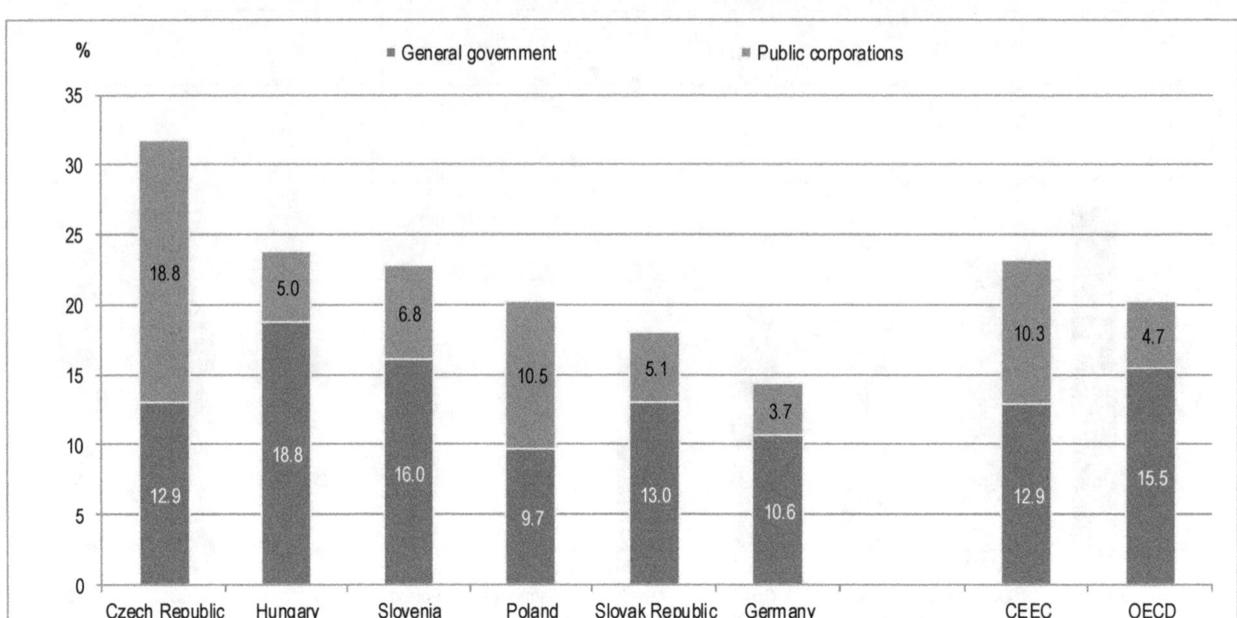

Note: Data on employment in public corporations for Austria are not available. Data for Germany are for 2010.

Source: ILO (2014a), *ILOSTAT* (database), www.ilo.org/ilostat; OECD (2014a), "Labour Force Statistics", *OECD Employment and Labour Market Statistics* (database), http://dx.doi.org/10.1787/lfs-lfs-data-en (accessed on 21 March 2015). Data for Hungary were provided by the National Statistical Office of Hungary.

StatLink http://dx.doi.org/10.1787/888933202765

Compensation of public sector employees

In 2012, the share of public spending allocated for the compensation of government employees was 20.6% in Hungary, which is comparable to its neighbouring countries, but lower than across the OECD (23.6%) (Figure 2.4). Between 2007 and 2012, cuts in public employment and reductions in salaries and benefits led to a decrease of the share of public expenditure dedicated to the compensation of general government employees in Hungary (-2.5 percentage points). This has also been the case in most neighbouring countries (except in Germany and Slovenia) and OECD countries. Apart from personnel reductions (through cuts and non-replacement of retiring staff), a series of measures were taken in Hungary to respond to the fiscal pressure, including abolishing the 13th month salary, reducing paid sick leave, reducing performance-related-pay/bonuses and pay freezes in nominal terms.

Figure 2.4. **Compensation of general government employees as a share of total public expenditure, Hungary, neighbouring countries and the OECD average, 2007 and 2012**

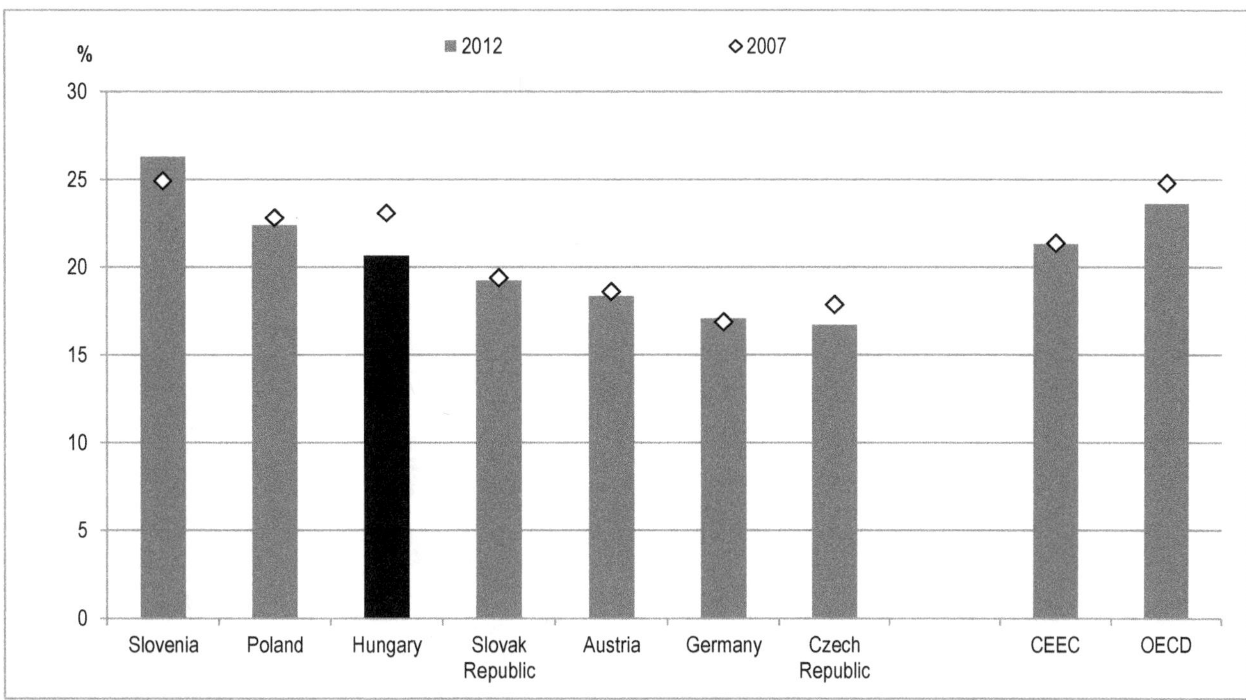

Source: OECD (2014b), *OECD National Accounts Statistics* (database), http://dx.doi.org/10.1787/na-data-en (accessed on 21 March 2015).

StatLink http://dx.doi.org/10.1787/888933202774

Distribution of employment across levels of government

In 2011, the central government in Hungary employed slightly more than one-third (36.2%) of all people working for governments (Figure 2.5). This is higher than in a federal country like Germany, but lower than in a smaller unitary country like Slovenia (in terms of geographic and population size). Compared to the Czech Republic (45.9%), the share of public employment in the central level of government in Hungary is relatively smaller and a bigger share of people works at the municipal level. However, data for the Czech Republic is from 2007 and recent reforms might have changed the distribution of employment across levels of government.

Figure 2.5. **Distribution of general government employment across levels of government, Hungary and some neighbouring countries, 2011**

	Central	Sub-central	Social security
Germany	12.9	78.5	8.7
Hungary	36.2	63.4	0.4
Czech Republic	45.9	53.0	1.1
Slovenia	58.9	38.2	2.8

Note: Data for Austria, Poland and the Slovak Republic are not available. Data for Germany are for 2010 rather than 2011. Data for the Czech Republic are for 2007 rather than 2011.

Source: ILO (2014b), *LABORSTA* (database), http://laborsta.ilo.org/. Data for Hungary were provided by the National Statistical Office of Hungary.

StatLink http://dx.doi.org/10.1787/888933202785

Since 2010, the share of people employed at the central level of government in Hungary has increased in absolute terms (Figure 2.6) and relative terms compared to the share of people employed in local governments. Between 2011 and 2012, employment at the central level increased by 11.6 percentage points, increasing from 36.2% to 47.8% of total general government employment. Employment in local governments decreased by the same magnitude, decreasing from 63.4% to 51.9% of total government employment.

Figure 2.6. **Evolution of the distribution of general government employment in Hungary, 2007-12**

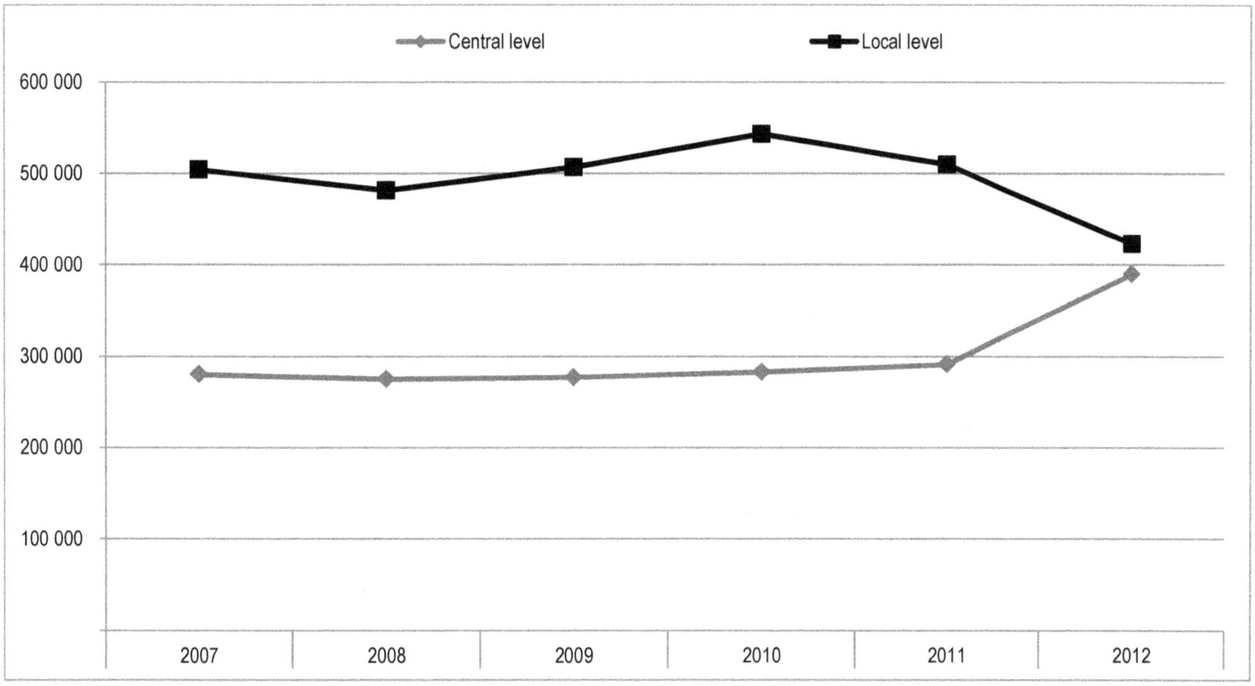

Source: National Statistical Office of Hungary.

StatLink http://dx.doi.org/10.1787/888933202790

The transfer from local to central government employment was driven mainly by a transfer of jobs in the health and social protection sectors (Figure 2.7). In 2012, the central government has taken responsibility for most of the financing and delivery of health care services and is now responsible for the entire hospital sector. Responsibilities for the management of social protection programmes have been transferred from the local governments to the central government. Responsibilities for economic development programmes were moved from the local to the central government with a significant increase in the number of people working on economic and labour affairs at the central level, which occurred in 2011. Finally the sectors of public order and safety (which was already very centralised) and education were also affected by the centralisation process, but to a smaller degree.

Figure 2.7. **Distribution of general government employment by sector in Hungary, 2010, 2011 and 2012**

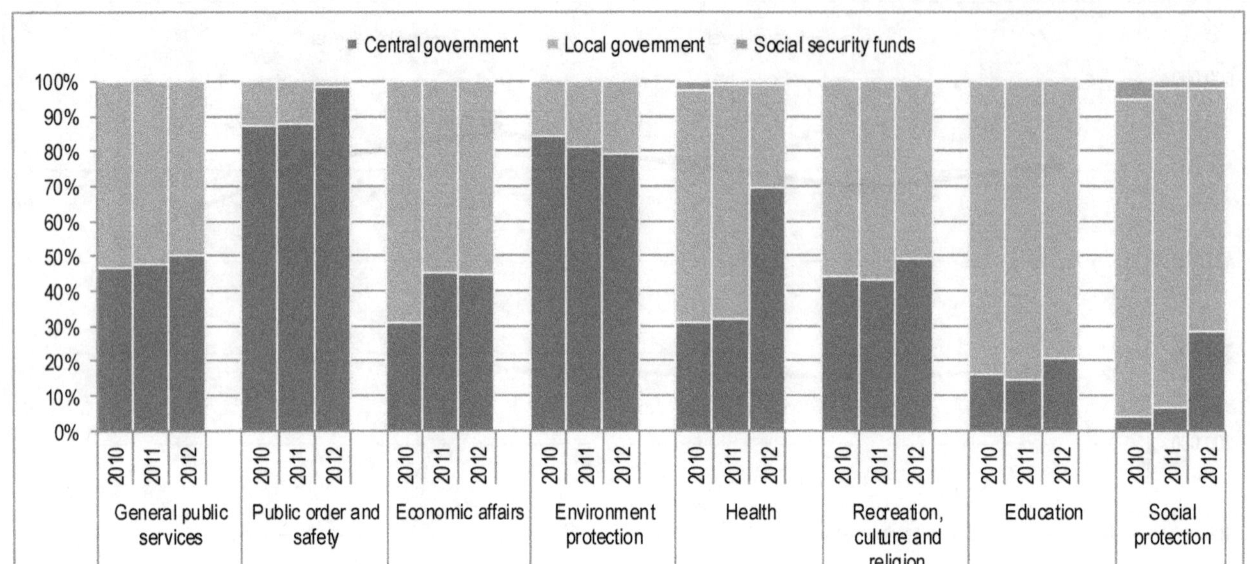

Source: National Statistical Office of Hungary.

StatLink http://dx.doi.org/10.1787/888933202800

Bibliography

Budapest Institute (2013), *Targeting and Impact Evaluation of EU-Funded Active Labour Market Programmes*, Budapest Institute for Policy Analysis, Budapest.

ILO (International Labour Organization) (2014a), *ILOSTAT* (database), www.ilo.org/ilostat.

ILO (2014b), *LABORSTA* (database), http://laborsta.ilo.org/.

OECD (2014a), "Labour Force Statistics", *OECD Employment and Labour Market Statistics* (database), http://dx.doi.org/10.1787/lfs-lfs-data-en (accessed on 21 March 2015).

OECD (2014b), *OECD National Accounts Statistics* (database), http://dx.doi.org/10.1787/na-data-en (accessed on 21 March 2015).

Chapter 3

Hungary's business environment and administrative burden

This chapter provides a set of indicators on the trends in administrative burden on businesses in Hungary. It uses mainly the most recent data from the OECD Product Market Regulation (PMR) indicators. The chapter sheds light on the barriers to entrepreneurship, the degree of complexity of regulatory procedures, administrative burdens on start-ups and the number of procedures and amount of time needed to start a company and comply with tax obligations.

One important pillar of the Magyary Program and 2014-2020 Public Sector Reform Strategy in Hungary concerns the simplification of the regulatory framework and the reduction of administrative burden and procedures for businesses. Hungary has achieved significant progress in improving some important aspects of the business environment in recent years, notably in reducing state control over private companies and reducing barriers to trade and investment. However, further efforts are required to reduce barriers to entrepreneurship, especially in the service sector, and notably to reduce the administrative burden in the time and cost involved in setting up new businesses in Hungary. Compared with its neighbouring countries, the number of procedures required to start a new business in Hungary is no longer greater, but takes much longer according to the Product Market Regulation (PMR) indicators. This suggests a need to further simplify these procedures. For existing companies, there is a need to continue to reduce the time and cost required to fulfil their tax obligations, which is much greater than in most other neighbouring countries and OECD countries.

Trends in the general business environment

Several instruments can be used to compare the quality of the business environment across countries. One of them is the OECD Product Market Regulation (PMR).[1] The PMR is a comprehensive and internationally comparable set of data about the state of regulation and market structures in OECD countries. The PMR uses a 0 to 6 point scale to assess and compare the "business-friendliness" of the environment in a given country: 0 represents the most business-friendly environment while 6 represents the least business-friendly (i.e. more state control and barriers). Based on the latest update of the PMR, the total average score of Hungary in 2013 was 1.3, which is better (lower) than the average score of other Central and Eastern European countries (CEEC). Compared to 2008, the average score of Hungary improved (fell) by 0.2 points, indicating that its business environment is progressively improving (Figure 3.1).

Barriers to entrepreneurship

The PMR is divided into three main categories: state control, barriers to entrepreneurship and barriers to trade and investment. While the scores of Hungary for state control and barriers to trade and investment compare favourably with other CEEC countries and the OECD average, its score for barriers to entrepreneurships (1.7) is relatively high compared to some neighbouring countries (Figure 3.2). There has been some progress in reducing barriers to entrepreneurship in Hungary since 2008, but the progress has not been as great as in Poland and the Slovak Republic.

Figure 3.1. **Product Market Regulation (average score), Hungary, neighbouring countries and the OECD average, 2008-13**

Composite Index 0-6 scale

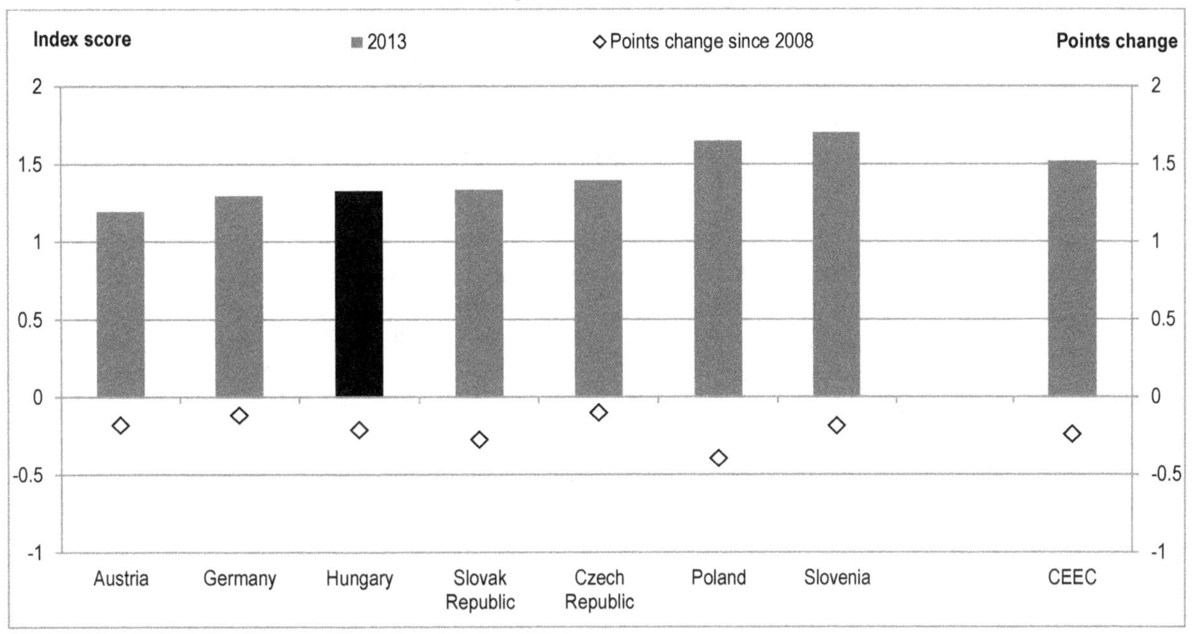

Note: A lower value indicates a better business environment.

Source: OECD (2014a), *OECD Product Market Regulation Statistics* (database), http://dx.doi.org/10.1787/pmr-data-en (accessed on 21 March 2015).

StatLink http://dx.doi.org/10.1787/888933202811

Figure 3.2. **Barriers to entrepreneurship, Hungary and neighbouring countries, 2008-13**

Composite Index 0-6 scale

Index score
Score in 2013 (left axis)
Points change since 2008 (right axis)
Points change
2
1.5
1
0.5
0
-0.5
-1
Slovak Republic
Austria
Poland
Germany
Hungary
Slovenia
Czech Republic
CEEC

Source: OECD (2014a), *OECD Product Market Regulation Statistics* (database), http://dx.doi.org/10.1787/pmr-data-en (accessed on 21 March 2015).

StatLink http://dx.doi.org/10.1787/888933202827

Complexity of regulatory procedures

Regulation is perhaps the most pervasive form of state intervention in economic activity. By establishing the "rules of the game" in a number of different areas – such as market competition, business conduct, consumer protection, public safety and health, and the environment – regulation is essential for the good working of market economies. One important issue for businesses, especially for businesses who are just starting their activity, is to get easy access to all the rules and regulations they will need to comply with.

In the PMR, ease of access to information about these rules and regulations is measured by a sub-indicator related to the complexity of regulatory procedures. A score of 0 corresponds to easy access and a score of 6 corresponds to a more complex way of displaying the information on rules and procedures for businesses. Hungary scores relatively well compared to its neighbouring countries and the OECD average on this aspect. In 2013, Hungary's score was 0.9, which is better (lower) than its neighbouring countries (except the Slovak Republic) and the CEEC average (Figure 3.3).

Figure 3.3. **Complexity of regulatory procedures (as a sub-indicator of barriers to entrepreneurship), Hungary and neighbouring countries, 2008-13**

Composite Index 0-6 scale

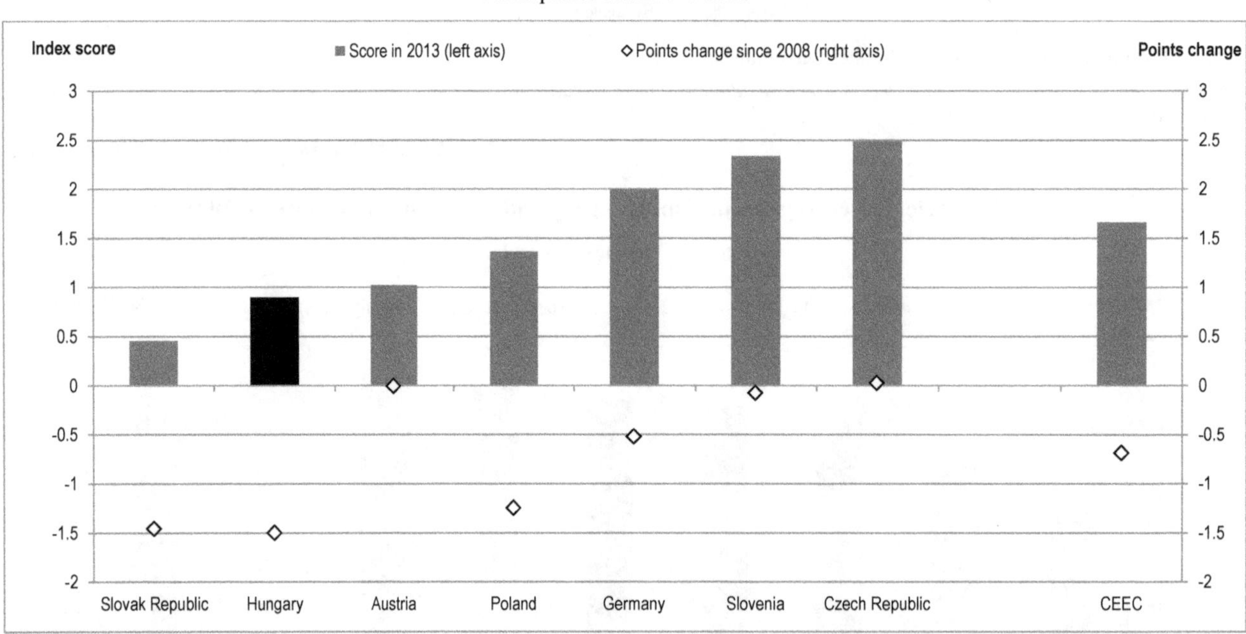

Source: OECD (2014a), *OECD Product Market Regulation Statistics* (database), http://dx.doi.org/10.1787/pmr-data-en (accessed on 21 March 2015).

StatLink http://dx.doi.org/10.1787/888933202830

Administrative burden on start-ups

Although important reforms have been implemented in recent years in Hungary to centralise the agencies responsible for delivering all the required licenses and permits and facilitate the processes for businesses when interacting with the public administration, the time and cost required to complete all the procedures remains much higher compared with its neighbouring countries and the OECD average. To give one concrete example, in 2013, the World Bank estimated that 24 procedures were required for businesses in Hungary to obtain a construction permit, against an average of 18 procedures in CEEC countries and 13 across the OECD (World Bank, 2014a).

Administrative burdens on start-ups (0 corresponding to least restrictive, 6 to most restrictive), which include the number of procedures, cost and time required to register a new company and get licenses, was 0.8 points higher in Hungary (at 2.7) than the average in CEEC countries (1.9) and the highest score among neighbouring countries (Figure 3.4).

Figure 3.4. **Administrative burdens on start-ups (as a sub-indicator of barriers to entrepreneurship), Hungary and neighbouring countries, 2008-13**

Composite Index 0-6 scale

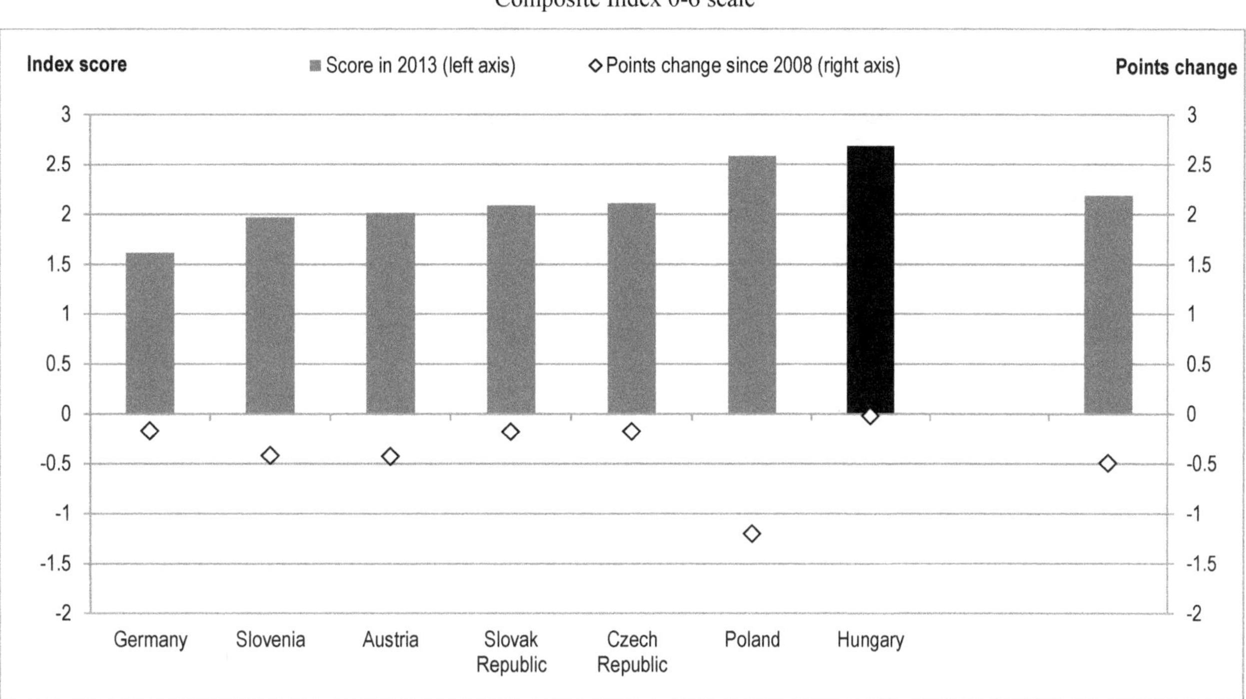

Source: OECD (2014a), *OECD Product Market Regulation Statistics* (database), http://dx.doi.org/10.1787/pmr-data-en (accessed on 21 March 2015).

StatLink http://dx.doi.org/10.1787/888933202845

In the past five years, administrative burdens on start-ups have remained high in Hungary while they have decreased in all of its neighbouring countries and across OECD countries on average. This is partly due to the persistence of barriers to entry in the service sector (Figure 3.5). The Hungarian government has recently taken several steps to further simplify administrative burden on start-ups in the service sector and align progressively with EU standards. The steps include implementing both a more flexible and transparent system for licensing in the construction sector and a new electronic licensing system for firms. In 2013, the Hungarian government also decided to simplify the system of requirements for professional services in order to create a more open labour market. The implementation is due in 2015 and should result in the simplification of almost 100 requirements for professional services.

Figure 3.5. **Barriers in the services sector (as a sub-indicator of barriers to entrepreneurship), Hungary and neighbouring countries, 2008-13**

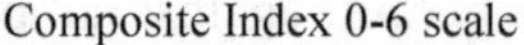

Composite Index 0-6 scale

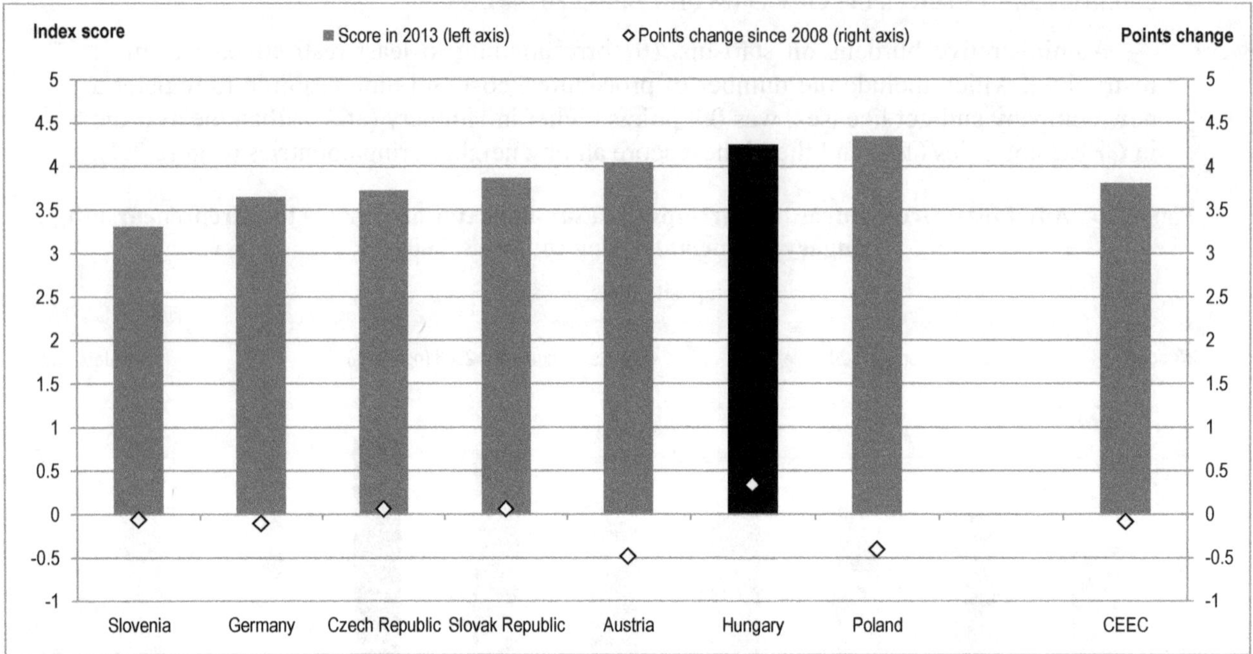

Source: OECD (2014a), *OECD Product Market Regulation Statistics* (database), http://dx.doi.org/10.1787/pmr-data-en (accessed on 21 March 2015).

StatLink http://dx.doi.org/10.1787/888933202853

While the number of mandatory procedures to register a company has been significantly reduced since 2008, the number of working days to complete these procedures (either to register an individual company[2] or a public limited company[3]) are generally higher than in other neighbouring countries according to the latest PMR data collection. For individual companies, the time required to complete procedures in Hungary is four times higher than in the Slovak Republic and the gap is even greater compared with other neighbouring countries (Figure 3.6). For public limited companies, which, in the case of Hungary, represent a relatively low proportion of newly created companies in 2013, the time required to complete all procedures (pre-registration and registration stages) is 35 working days, which is greater than in most neighbouring countries (except Poland).

Figure 3.6. **Number of procedures, typical time needed and number of people to contact when registering a company, Hungary and neighbouring countries, 2013**

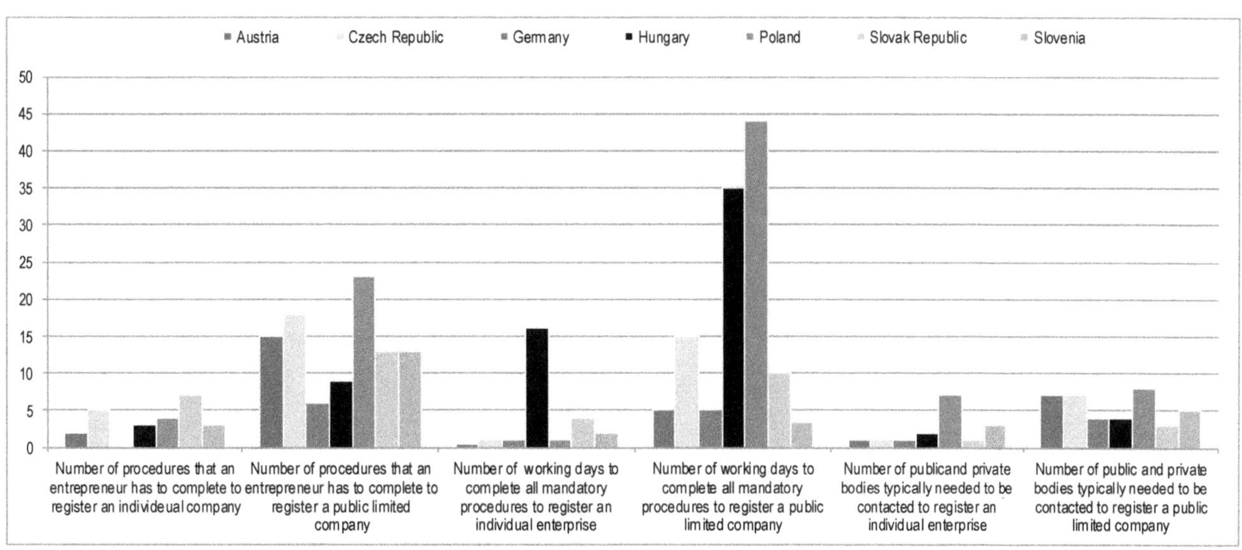

Note: "Typical" refers to the average time involved in setting up a business entity entirely through the most widely used process of registration. Data come from the OECD Regulatory Indicators Questionnaire 2013 and answers were provided by member country representatives. Users of PMR data should be aware that this data may no longer fully reflect the current situation in fast reforming countries. Depending on the countries, the two categories of companies defined in the PMR apply to a limited share of the total number of newly created companies.

Source: OECD (2014a), *OECD Product Market Regulation Statistics* (database), http://dx.doi.org/10.1787/pmr-data-en (accessed on 21 March 2015).

StatLink http://dx.doi.org/10.1787/888933202861

The picture is somewhat different when using a broader definition of companies (limited not only to the two categories included in the PMR, which may not cover the full range of newly created companies) and when focussing on small and medium-sized enterprises (SMEs) with limited liability operating only in the largest business city of an economy - as the World Bank's *Doing Business* methodology does. Based on expert and local businesses' judgements, the number of procedures required to start a company (any type) falls to four procedures, while the time required falls to five days, which is below the CEEC and OECD average (Figure 3.7).

The cost of starting a business in Hungary, as a percentage of the average income per capita, is relatively high. In the World Bank methodology, it includes all official fees and fees for legal or professional services if such services are required by law. In 2013, the estimated cost of starting a company in Hungary was equal to 8.6% of the average income per capita, which is 2.6 percentage points more than the CEEC average and more than twice the OECD average (3.6%). Only in Poland is the cost of starting a business higher (Figure 3.8).

Figure 3.7. **Number of procedures and time required to start a business (limited liability) in the largest business city of an economy, Hungary, neighbouring countries and OECD average, 2013**

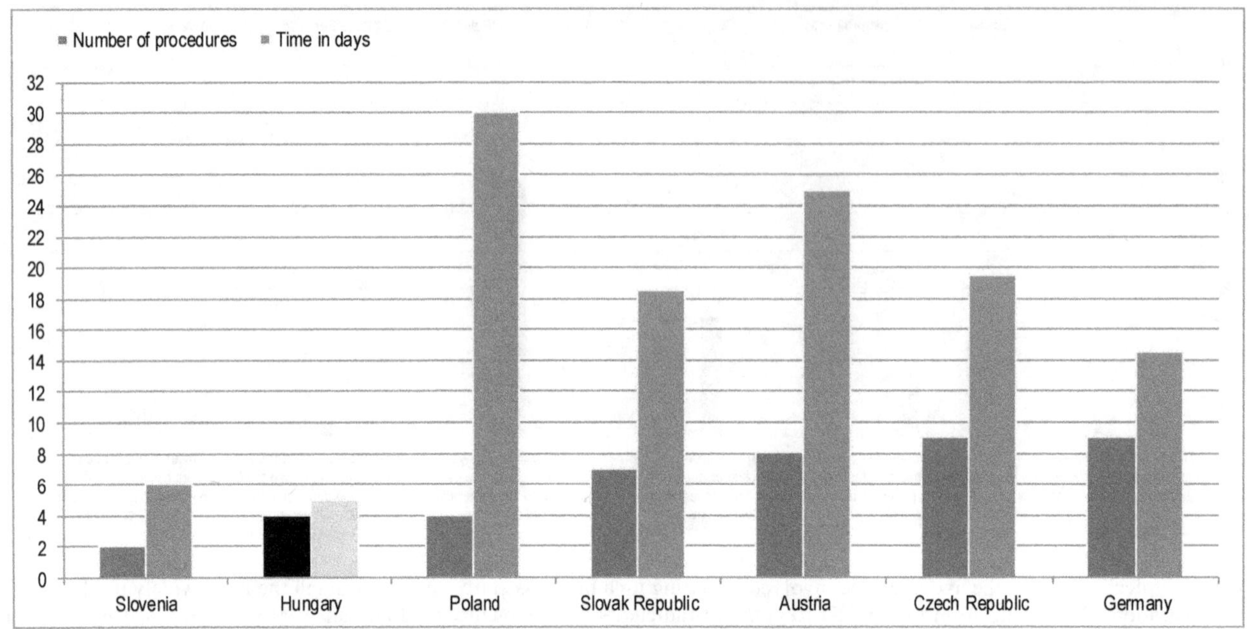

Note: Countries are ranked based on the number of procedures (from lowest to highest).

Source: World Bank (2014b), Ease of Doing Business Index, http://data.worldbank.org/indicator/IC.BUS.EASE.XQ.

StatLink http://dx.doi.org/10.1787/888933202872

Figure 3.8. **Cost of starting a business (limited liability) in the largest business city of an economy, Hungary, neighbouring countries and the OECD average, 2013**

% of average income per capita

Note: In Slovenia, there is no official fee required by the law to start a business.

Source: World Bank (2014b), Ease of Doing Business Index, http://data.worldbank.org/indicator/IC.BUS.EASE.XQ.

StatLink http://dx.doi.org/10.1787/888933202888

Burden of tax payments

For businesses already in place, the time required to pay their taxes and social security contributions to the government has decreased since 2007, but is still significantly higher than in other OECD countries. According to *Paying Taxes 2014* (World Bank, IFC and PwC, 2014), a Hungarian SME spends 277 hours per year complying with their tax obligations, 50% more than the OECD average (Figure 3.9). In 2013, the administrative costs of tax collection, either relative to GDP per capita or to tax revenue, was also high compared with other countries (OECD, 2013b). This is due mainly to a high number of different and special taxes that are often complex and have regularly changed over past years (OECD, 2014b).

Some of the recent special taxes introduced by the government were mostly paid by large enterprises that are already closely monitored by the tax authorities, and should not further raise the cost of collecting taxes in Hungary. Some optional, simplified tax schemes were also introduced in 2013, with the firm intention to reduce the complexity of the tax system and reduce administrative and tax burdens on SMEs in future years.

Figure 3.9. **Time taken to prepare, file and pay taxes, Hungary, neighbouring countries and the OECD average, 2007-13**

Number of hours per year

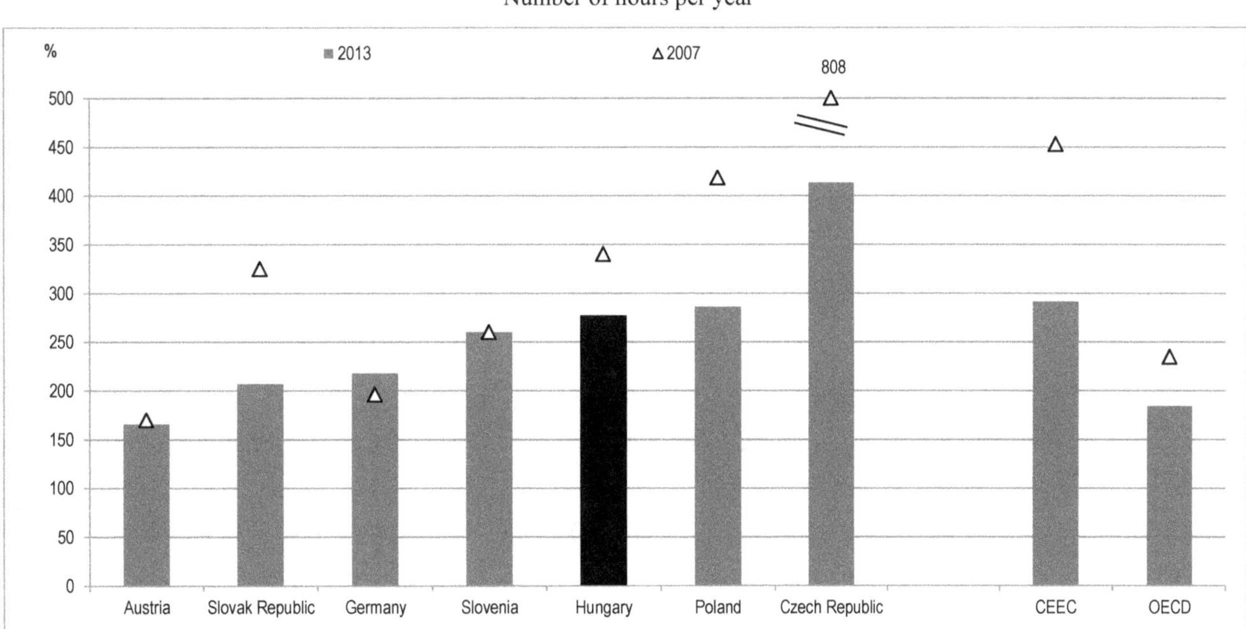

Source: World Bank, IFC and PwC (2014), *Paying Taxes 2014: The global picture*, www.doingbusiness.org/reports/thematic-reports/~/media/GIAWB/Doing%20Business/Documents/Special-Reports/Paying-Taxes-2014.pdf.

StatLink http://dx.doi.org/10.1787/888933202899

Notes

1. The Product Market Regulation data measure the economy-wide regulatory and market environments in 34 OECD countries in (or around) 1998, 2003, 2008 and 2013. They are consistent across time and countries. Users of the data should be aware that this data may no longer fully reflect the current situation in fast reforming countries.
2. An individual enterprise is defined as an enterprise in which the owner is solely responsible for business liabilities, which are unlimited and extend to private assets (OECD, 2013a).
3. A public limited company is defined as an incorporated legal entity separate and independent of the owners or shareholders. Liability of the company is limited to the extent of its assets and individual shareholder liability is limited to the amount of capital contributed. A public limited company can raise capital through public subscriptions and can be listed on public debt and equity markets. There are no limits on the number of shareholders (OECD, 2013a).

Bibliography

OECD (2014a), *OECD Product Market Regulation Statistics* (database), http://dx.doi.org/10.1787/pmr-data-en (accessed on 21 March 2015).

OECD (2014b), *OECD Economic Surveys: Hungary 2014*, OECD Publishing, Paris, http://dx.doi.org/10.1787/eco_surveys-hun-2014-en.

OECD (2013a), "The OECD Regulatory Indicators Questionnaire 2013", www.oecd.org/eco/reform/PMR-Questionnaire-2013.pdf.

OECD (2013b), *Tax Administration 2013: Comparative Information on OECD and Other Advanced and Emerging Economies*, OECD Publishing, Paris, http://dx.doi.org/10.1787/9789264200814-en.

World Bank (2014a), *Doing Business Report: Understanding regulations for small and medium-sized companies*, 11th edition, World Bank, Washington.

World Bank (2014b), Ease of Doing Business Index, http://data.worldbank.org/indicator/IC.BUS.EASE.XQ.

World Bank, IFC and PwC (2014), *Paying Taxes 2014: The global picture*, www.doingbusiness.org/reports/thematic-reports/~/media/GIAWB/Doing%20Business/Documents/Special-Reports/Paying-Taxes-2014.pdf.

Chapter 4

Electronic delivery of government services in Hungary

This chapter reviews the use of digital government services by citizens and businesses in Hungary. It focusses on both simple interactions (e.g. finding information on government websites) and more complex interactions (filing forms on line). Some breakdowns are provided for different categories of citizens (by age group, education level) and by size of company. The chapter also takes a look at a more specific type of digital government service – electronic procurement systems – and their degree of usage by companies in Hungary compared to neighbouring countries.

Digital government can raise public sector efficiency and can improve the timeliness of public service delivery for citizens and businesses. This chapter reviews the use of digital government services by citizens and businesses in Hungary. Three main findings are discussed:

1. The level of e-government uptake among citizens and businesses is comparable to its neighbouring countries, but is slightly below the EU average.
2. There remain some disparities in the use of e-government services, by age for citizens, and by size of companies.
3. Despite efforts made by the Hungarian government to provide more information and services on line on public procurement, the use of e-procurement systems by companies is still limited in Hungary, and well below the Central and Eastern European country (CEEC) and EU average.

Citizen use of online platforms to interact with the government

In 2013, exactly half (50%) of Hungarian citizens reported having used the Internet in the past 12 months to interact with public authorities (Figure 4.1). This is higher than the CEEC average (46%), but lower than the EU average (54%). Regarding more advanced types of interactions, 23% of Hungarians reported having filled in forms addressed to the authorities through the Internet in the past 12 months, compared to 18% on average in the CEEC region and 27% across the EU. The use of the Internet to submit completed forms is higher in Hungary (23%) than in the Slovak Republic (19%), Germany (17%), Poland (17%) and the Czech Republic (9%), but lower than in Slovenia (28%) and Austria (34%).

Figure 4.1. **Citizens using the Internet to interact with public authorities by type of activity, Hungary, neighbouring countries and the EU average, 2013**

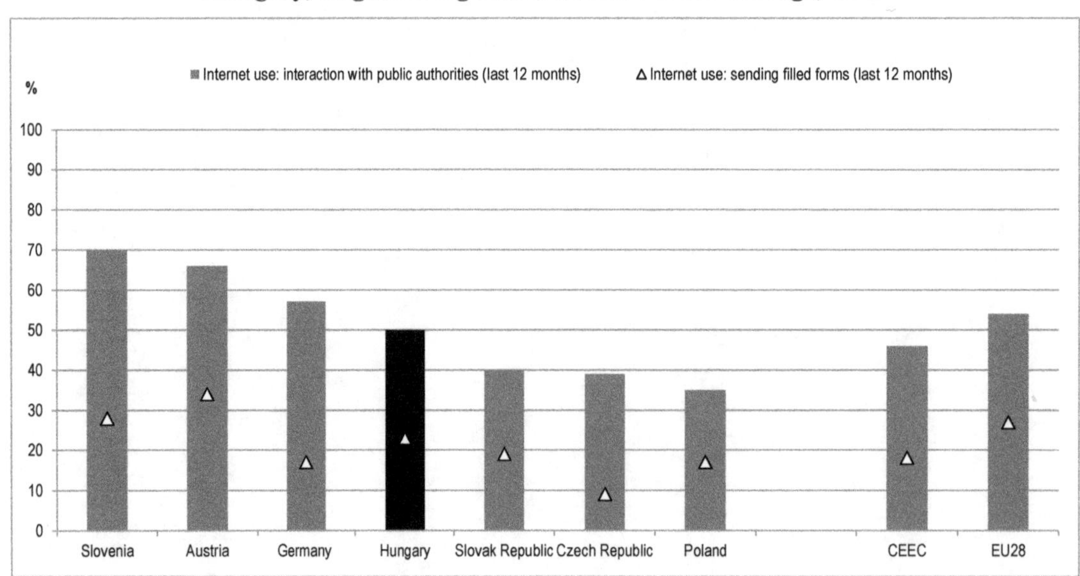

Note: Data refer to the percentage of citizens having used the Internet in the past 12 months, for any kind of purpose.

Source: Eurostat (2014), *Information Society Statistics* (database), http://ec.europa.eu/eurostat/web/information-society/data/database.

StatLink http://dx.doi.org/10.1787/888933202905

Disparities in the use of e-government services

Across the OECD, disparities generally persist in the use of e-government services depending on the age of citizens and their level of education. In Hungary, as in most CEEC countries, the age group which reports the highest level of interaction with their government via the Internet is younger people aged 35 to 44 years old (56%). However, compared to most of its neighbouring countries, the gap between the use of online services by Hungarians aged 35-44 years old versus older people (e.g. 65-74 years old) is less pronounced (Figure 4.2).

Figure 4.2. **Citizens using the Internet to interact with governments by age group, Hungary, neighbouring countries and the EU average, 2013**

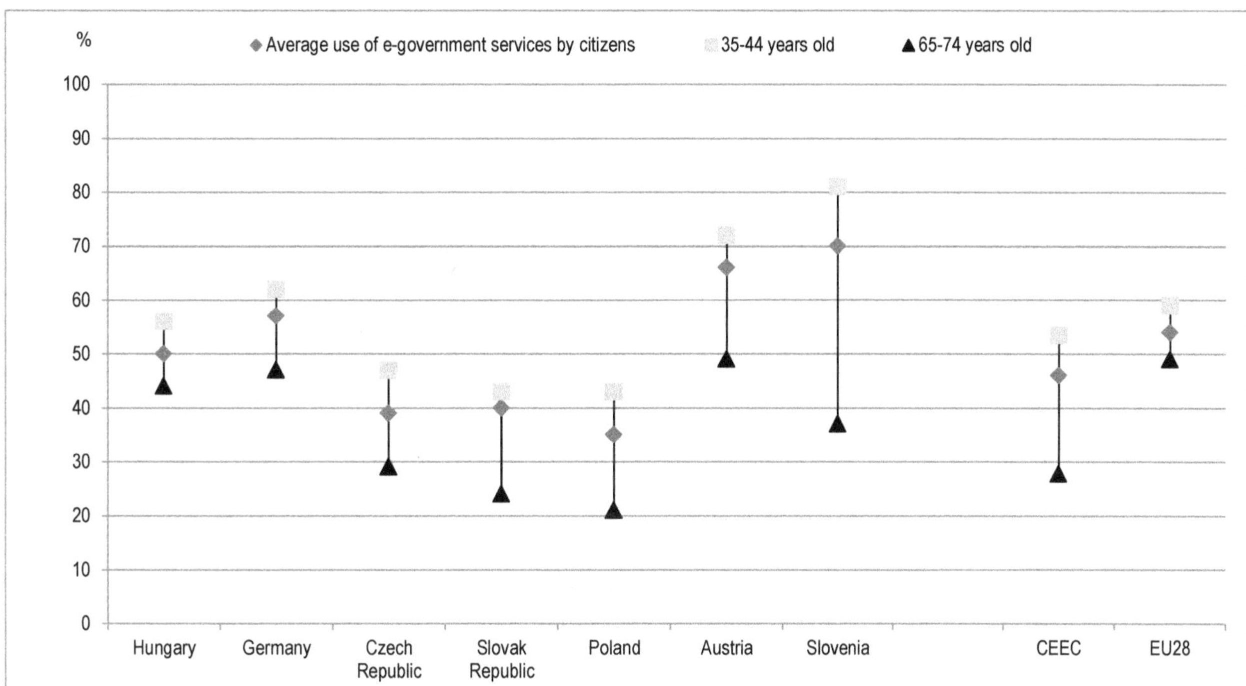

Note: Data refer to the percentage of citizens having used the Internet in the past 12 months, for any kind of purpose.

Source: Eurostat (2014), *Information Society Statistics* (database), http://ec.europa.eu/eurostat/web/information-society/data/database

StatLink http://dx.doi.org/10.1787/888933202916

Regarding disparities by education level, well-educated people tend to use online services more often to interact with their government in all OECD countries. In 2013, more than three-quarters (77%) of people aged 25 to 54 with a high level of education in Hungary reported having used the Internet to interact with the government in the past 12 months, compared with one-quarter (25%) for people with a low level of education (Figure 4.3). The gap between the most educated and least educated people in the use of online services is relatively more significant in Hungary (52 percentage points) than the average across CEEC countries (45 percentage points) and EU countries (33 percentage points). This is due in part to the lower level of Internet connectivity among people with a low level of education in Hungary. But it might also suggest that people with a lower level of education communicate less with the government, are less aware of the possibility to use public online services for different purposes, or do not have the sufficient skills to use those services.

Figure 4.3. **Citizens using the Internet to interact with public authorities by education level, Hungary, neighbouring countries and the EU average, 2013**

◆ Average use of e-government services by citizens ■ Individuals aged 25 to 54 with low formal education ▲ Individuals aged 25 to 54 with high formal education

%

100
75
50
25
0

Slovenia Austria Germany Hungary Slovak Republic Czech Republic Poland CEEC EU28

Note: Data refer to the percentage of citizens having used the Internet in the past 12 months, for any kind of purpose.

Source: Eurostat (2014), *Information Society Statistics* (database), http://ec.europa.eu/eurostat/web/information-society/data/database.

StatLink http://dx.doi.org/10.1787/888933202921

For the first time in 2013, Eurostat also collected data on citizen satisfaction with e-government websites. Box 4.1 and Figure 4.4 set out the results of this exercise.

Uptake of e-government services by businesses

Facilitating access for businesses to information and to online services is a means for governments to support the private sector by facilitating "doing business" and reducing the administrative burden. In 2011, 83% of all companies in Hungary reported having used the Internet in the past 12 months to interact with the government (Figure 4.5). This is lower than in all other CEEC countries and the OECD average (88%).

Regarding more advanced types of interactions with government, 45% of Hungarian businesses reported having handled an administrative procedure completely electronically, compared with an average of 53% in CEEC countries and 55% across the OECD. The use of online services by businesses to carry out an administrative procedure is higher in Hungary than in Poland, but lower than in the Czech Republic, the Slovak Republic and Slovenia (where it reaches 74%).

Box 4.1. **Satisfaction of Hungarian citizens with e-government websites**

For the first time in 2013, Eurostat collected data on the satisfaction of Hungarian citizens with e-government websites in the context of the 2011-15 benchmarking framework (endorsed by the i2010 High Level Group in November 2009) for the Digital Agenda Scoreboard. The results of the survey show that in Hungary, 44% of citizens reported that they were satisfied with the ease of finding the information they were looking for on line (Figure 4.4). The same percentage of people reported being satisfied with the usefulness of the information made available by the government. Regarding online services (such as purchasing a birth certificate, renewing a driver's license and vehicle registration, and online tax submission), 39% of Hungarians reported being satisfied with the ease of using these services on line. In addition, 35% of Hungarians reported being satisfied with the information they received following an information request to the government via the Internet. The satisfaction level of citizens with these government websites in Hungary was generally lower than in Slovenia, but higher than in the Slovak Republic and Poland.

Figure 4.4. **Level of satisfaction of Hungarian citizens with e-government websites, 2013**

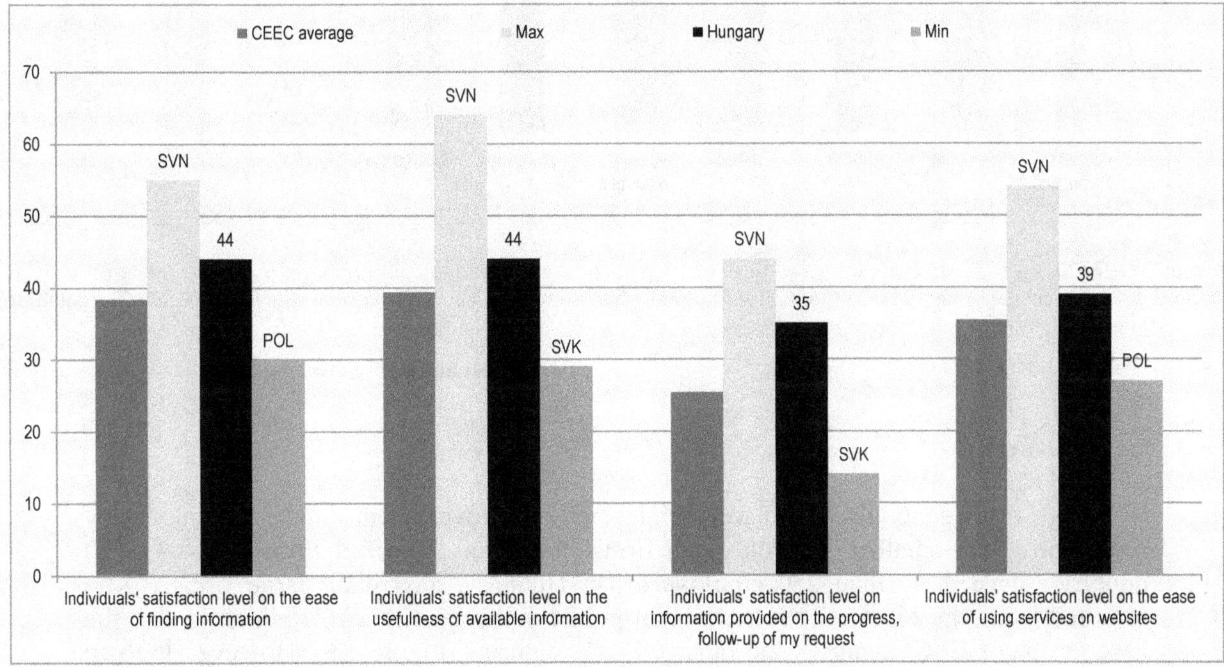

Note: Data refers to the percentage of citizens having used the Internet in the past 12 months, for any kind of purpose.

Source: Eurostat (2014), *Information Society Statistics* (database), http://ec.europa.eu/eurostat/web/information-society/data/database.

StatLink http://dx.doi.org/10.1787/888933202933

Figure 4.5. **Firms using the Internet to interact with public authorities by type of activity, Hungary, neighbouring countries and the EU average, 2011**

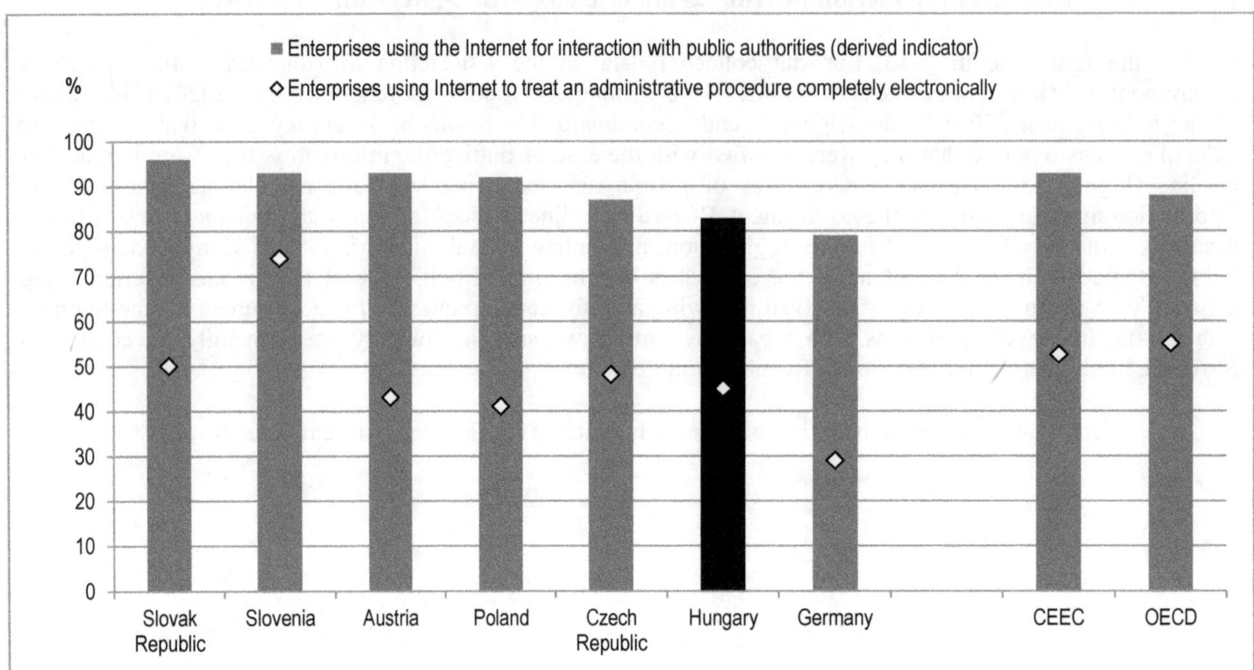

Source: OECD (2014), *ICT Database*, www.oecd-ilibrary.org/science-and-technology/information-and-communication-technology-ict/ (accessed on 21st March 2015); and Eurostat (2014), *Information Society Statistics* (database), http://ec.europa.eu/eurostat/web/information-society/data/database.

StatLink http://dx.doi.org/10.1787/888933202943

Disparities in the use of e-government, by firm size

Large firms generally have a very high level of e-government uptake, although they represent a very small proportion of all firms (less than 1% of all firms across OECD countries have more than 250 employees). In Hungary, almost all large firms (98%) reported using the Internet to interact with public authorities in 2011, which is also the case in other CEEC countries and other OECD countries (Figure 4.6). However, the gap is relatively greater in Hungary in the use of e-services by large firms and small enterprises. E-government uptake among small enterprises was only 81%, compared with 90% on average across CEEC countries and 88% across the OECD. Greater efforts to facilitate access and use of online services by small enterprises in Hungary may help them achieve savings in terms of time and cost, reduce administrative burden and promote their survival and expansion.

Figure 4.6. **Firms using the Internet to interact with government by firm size, Hungary, neighbouring countries and the OECD average, 2012**

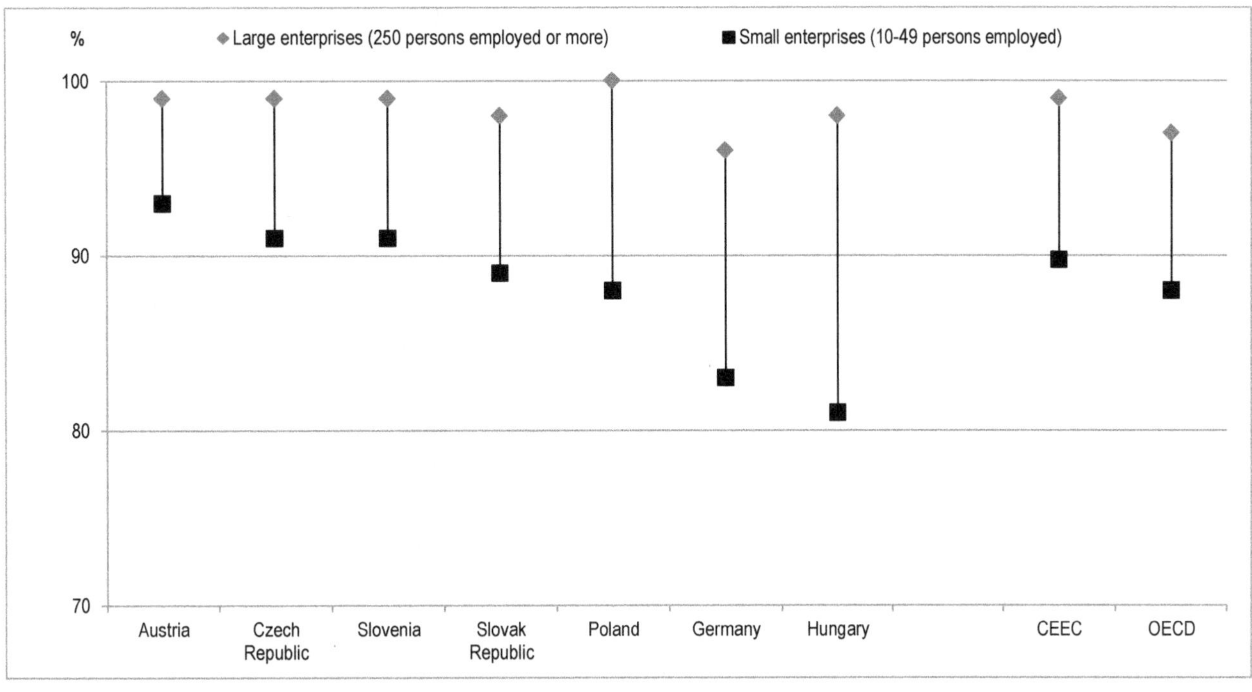

Source: OECD (2014), *ICT Database*, www.oecd-ilibrary.org/science-and-technology/information-and-communication-technology-ict/ (accessed on 21st March 2015); and Eurostat (2014), *Information Society Statistics* (database), http://ec.europa.eu/eurostat/web/information-society/data/database.

StatLink http://dx.doi.org/10.1787/888933202958

Use of e-procurement systems

The size of government procurement in Hungary accounts for about one-quarter of total general government expenditures every year (26% in 2011). According to the 2013 Special Eurobarometer 397 report on corruption, 47% of Hungarian respondents considered that corruption was widespread in public procurement managed by central authorities (against 56% on average across the EU). Among the most widespread practices identified, Hungarian businesses stated that specifications were tailor made for specific companies (64%), that there was collusive bidding (58%) and unclear selection or evaluation criteria (48%) (European Commission, 2013). These perception indicators illustrate some risk factors and vulnerabilities on public procurement practices and procedures that call for further efforts to raise transparency and competition in this area.

The use of information and communication technologies in public procurement can facilitate access to public tenders, increase competition and can help reduce government costs by reducing administrative burden, shortening procurement contract cycles and raising compliance levels. In 2011, 19% of Hungarian companies used e-procurement systems to access tender documents on line (Figure 4.7). In 2013, this proportion did not increase, but rather decreased slightly to 18%. This trend is running counter to what has happened in most other CEEC countries and EU countries, where the share of companies using e-procurement systems continues to grow.

Figure 4.7. **Percentage of companies using e-procurement systems to access tender documents, Hungary, neighbouring countries and the EU average, 2011-13**

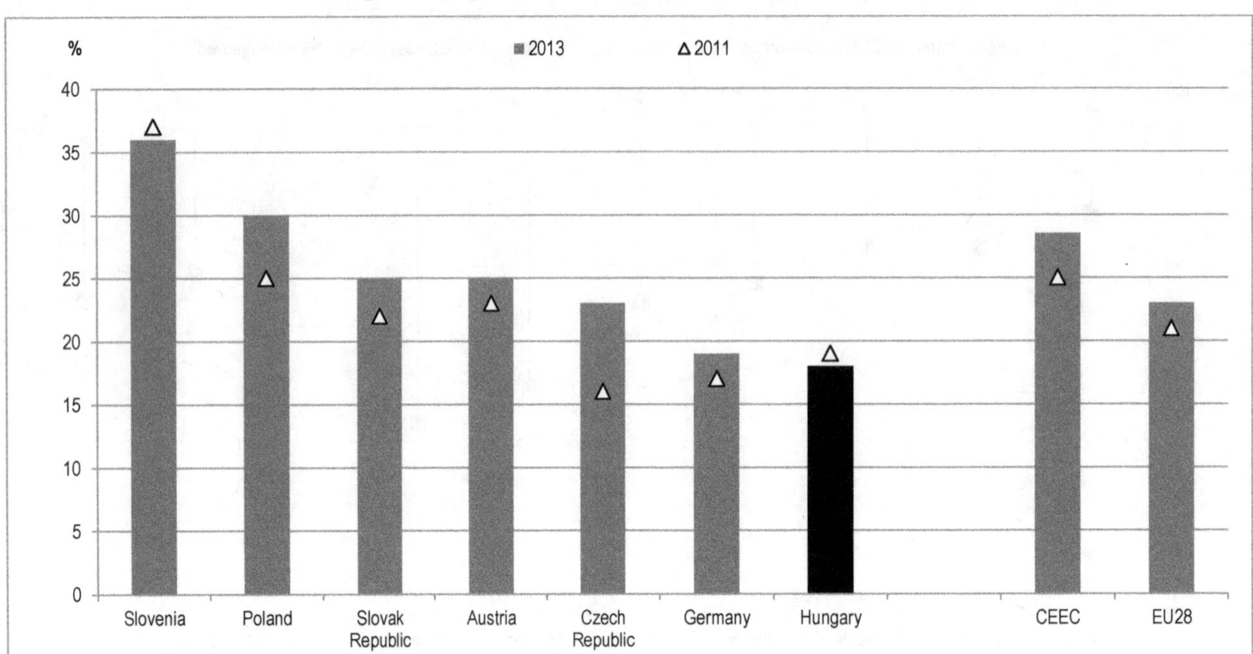

Source: Eurostat (2014), *Information Society Statistics* (database), http://ec.europa.eu/eurostat/web/information-society/data/database.

StatLink http://dx.doi.org/10.1787/888933202968

In January 2012, a new Public Procurement Act (PPA) entered into force in Hungary with additional amendments adopted in June 2013. Contracting authorities must now publish information on negotiated procedures that take place without publication of contract notices on their websites. The Public Procurement database was also broadened. However, there is no concrete and effective sanctioning mechanism if those obligations are not met and it is still not mandatory to disclose all types of public procurements documents (including, e.g. detailed evaluation forms). Research conducted by Transparency International concluded that about 40% of examined Hungarian municipalities did not publish any data on their websites concerning their 2012 public procurements (Transparency International Hungary, 2013). This calls for a more integrated and whole-of-government approach to raise transparency and competition in public procurement at all levels of government.

Bibliography

European Commission (2013), *Special Eurobarometer 397: Corruption*, Directorate-General for Home Affairs, Brussels, http://ec.europa.eu/public_opinion/archives/ebs/ebs_397_en.pdf.

Eurostat (2014), *Information Society Statistics* (database), http://ec.europa.eu/eurostat/web/information-society/data/database.

OECD (2014), *ICT Database*, www.oecd-ilibrary.org/science-and-technology/information-and-communication-technology-ict/ (accessed on 21st March 2015).

Transparency International Hungary (2013), *Procurement Publicity in Hungary*, Budapest.

Chapter 5

Government performance and the health care system in Hungary

This chapter provides a set of indicators related to the performance of the health care system in Hungary. It provides indicators on the general level of satisfaction of the population with health care services, on the evolution of life expectancy and on the evolution of public and private spending on health care. It also sets out measures of access to care, unmet care needs by income level and a series of indicators on the efficiency of the health care system in Hungary.

This chapter focusses on the performance of the health care system in Hungary, an important aspect covered by government reforms in Hungary. It finds that public satisfaction with the health care system in Hungary has increased in recent years, but remains below satisfaction levels in many of its neighbouring countries and below the average across OECD countries. Hungary spends slightly less on health than most of its neighbouring countries, but a large part of its spending is allocated to hospital care and pharmaceutical spending, leaving only a small share of resources allocated for disease prevention and the delivery of primary care outside hospitals. Access to care has been an issue for people in low-income groups and people living in rural areas, although the Hungarian government has recently taken measures to improve access to care for people in rural regions. Efficiency in health care delivery may also be improved by strengthening efforts to reduce unnecessary hospital admissions and unnecessarily long lengths of stay, and by taking further steps to reduce pharmaceutical spending.

Citizen satisfaction with the availability of quality health care

Citizen satisfaction with the health care system increased in Hungary between 2007 and 2013, rising from 54% to 60% of the population reporting that they were satisfied with the availability and quality of health services. Still, this satisfaction rate lags behind the satisfaction levels in many of its neighbouring countries (for example, in Slovenia, where public satisfaction is over 80%) and the OECD average (above 70%) (Figure 5.1).

Figure 5.1. **Public satisfaction with the health care system, Hungary, neighbouring countries and the OECD average, 2007-13**

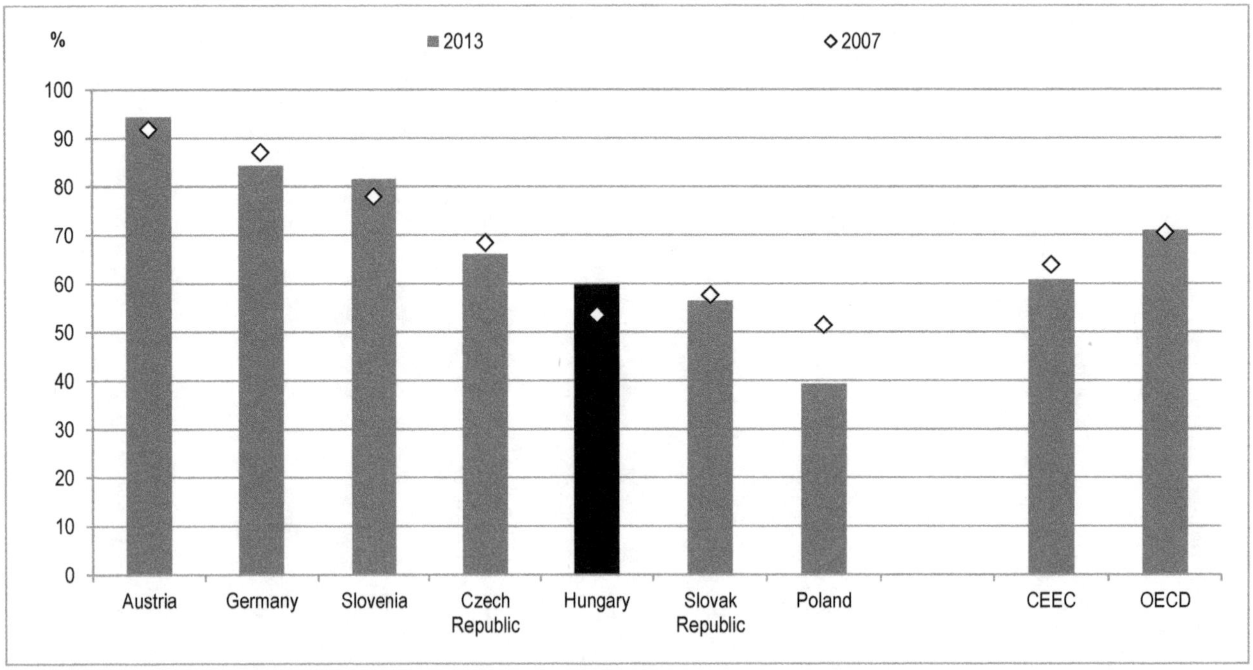

Note: Data refer to the percentage of respondents reporting being satisfied when answering the question, "In the city or area where you live, are you satisfied or dissatisfied with the availability of quality health care?" Data for some OECD countries are for 2006 (rather than 2007) and 2011 (rather than 2013).

Source: Gallup World Poll, www.gallup.com

StatLink http://dx.doi.org/10.1787/888933202975

While some of the health care reforms carried out in Hungary between 2007 and 2013 have contributed to improving the availability and quality of health services, the data show that there continues to be certain issues related to access to health services and efficiency in health care spending.

Evolution of life expectancy since 2000

Many factors affect life expectancy beyond access to quality health services, including the living and working conditions of the population, unhealthy behaviours (smoking, harmful alcohol drinking, poor nutrition habits, physical inactivity) and the physical environment (e.g. air pollution).

In 2012, life expectancy at birth in Hungary was 75.2 years, which is one year below the Slovak Republic, three years below the Czech Republic, and a full five years below Slovenia and the OECD average (Figure 5.2). Since 2000, life expectancy in Hungary has increased significantly (+3.3 years), but the gap with other Central and Eastern European countries (CEEC) has remained the same.

Figure 5.2. **Life expectancy at birth, Hungary, neighbouring countries and the OECD average, all populations, 2000-12**

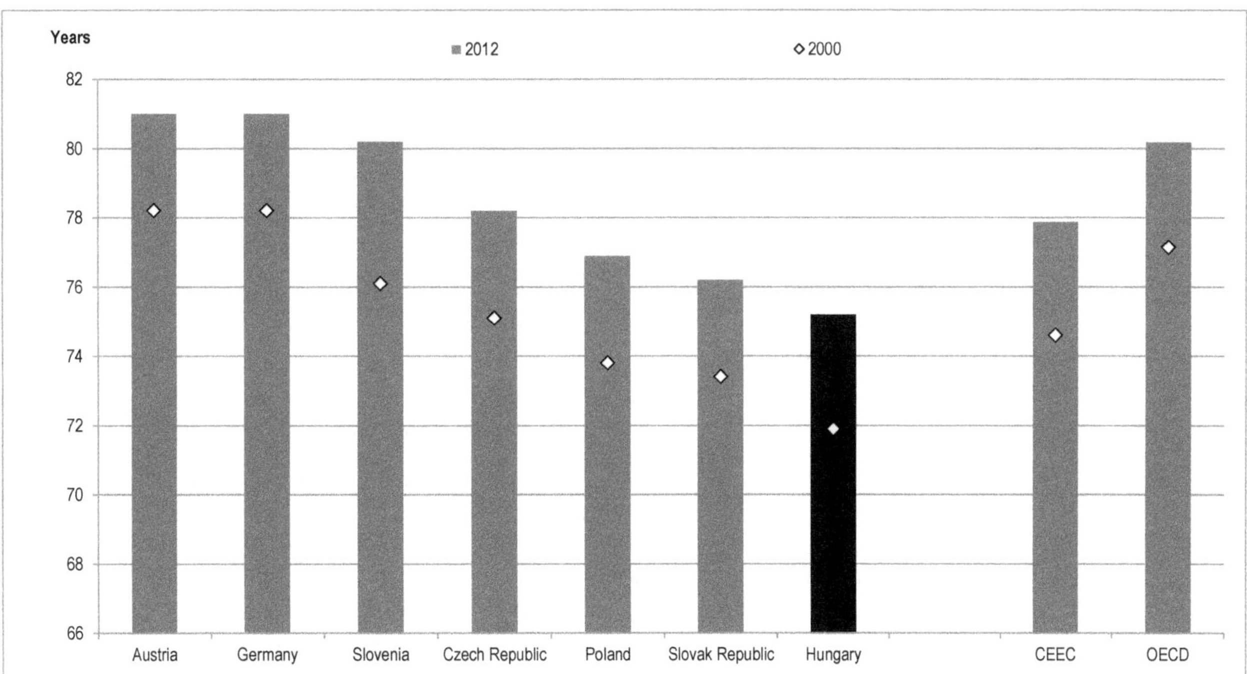

Source: OECD (2014a), *OECD Health Statistics* (database), http://dx.doi.org/10.1787/health-data-en (accessed on 21 March 2015).

StatLink http://dx.doi.org/10.1787/888933202986

A simple correlation between life expectancy and health spending per capita indicates that Hungary has a lower life expectancy than what might be "predicted" given its level of health spending (Figure 5.3). As already noted, life expectancy is affected by a range of factors, including many that are beyond the health care system. Still, this simple correlation suggests that there might be opportunities to improve the performance of the Hungarian health system in terms of access, quality and efficiency, in order to improve health services and life expectancy.

Figure 5.3. **Life expectancy at birth and total expenditure on health per capita, Hungary, neighbouring countries and OECD countries, 2012**

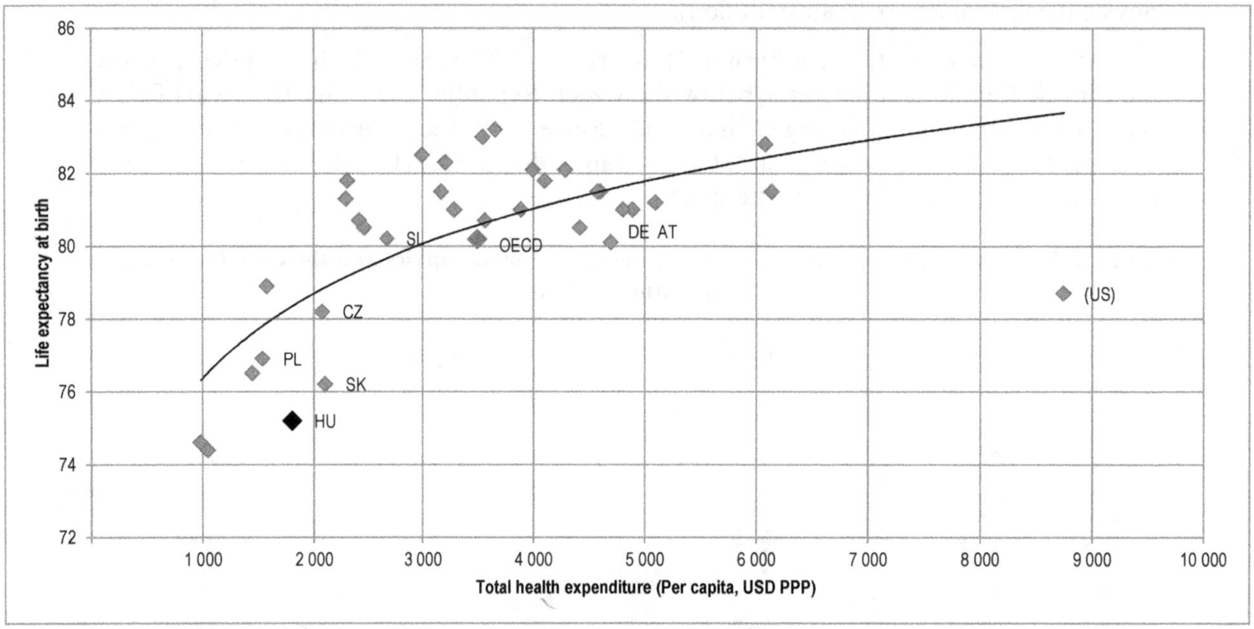

Source: OECD (2014a), *OECD Health Statistics* (database), http://dx.doi.org/10.1787/health-data-en (accessed on 21 March 2015).

StatLink http://dx.doi.org/10.1787/888933202992

Health expenditure per capita

Health expenditure in Hungary accounted for 8.0% of GDP in 2012, significantly less than the OECD average of 9.3%, but equal to the Slovak Republic and higher than in the Czech Republic and Poland. On a per capita basis, health spending in Hungary was just over half of the OECD average in 2012, with spending of USD 1 803 in 2012 (adjusted for purchasing power parity), compared with an OECD average of USD 3 484 (Figure 5.4). Health spending per capita in Hungary is higher than in Poland, but slightly lower than in the Czech Republic and the Slovak Republic, and much lower than in Slovenia.

Figure 5.4. **Health expenditure per capita, Hungary, neighbouring countries and the OECD average, 2012**

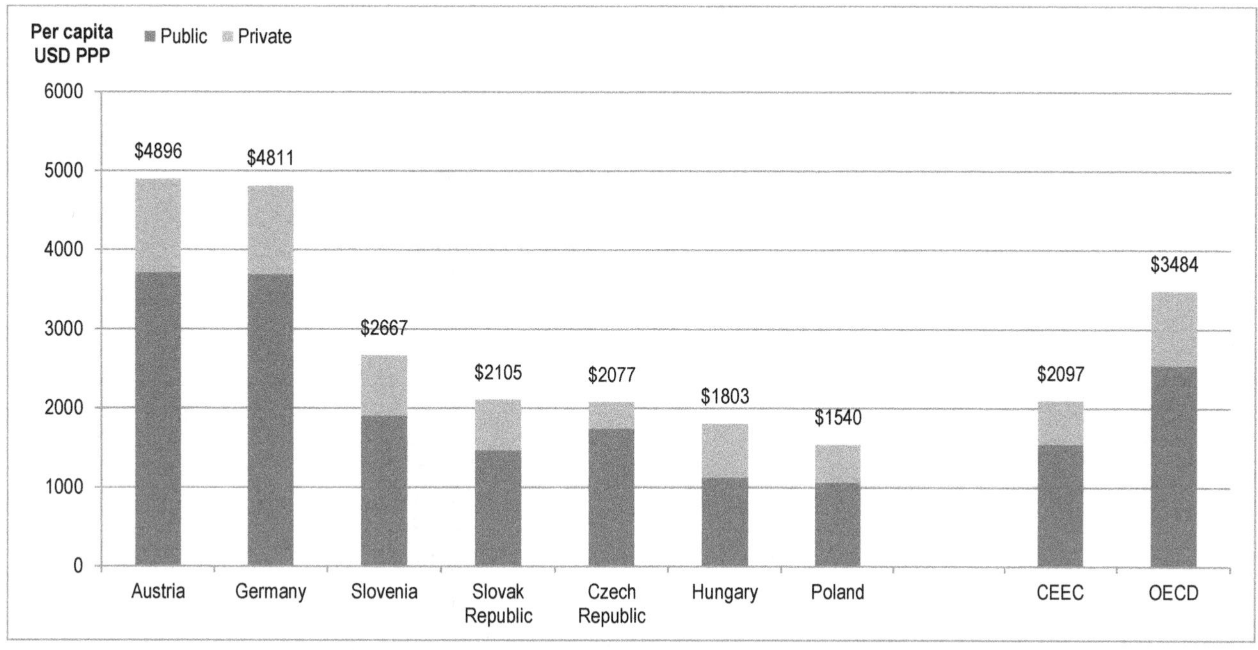

Source: OECD (2014a), *OECD Health Statistics* (database), http://dx.doi.org/10.1787/health-data-en (accessed on 21 March 2015).

StatLink http://dx.doi.org/10.1787/888933203000

Only 62% of the total health expenditure in Hungary was financed by public funds (general government and social security) in 2012, which is much lower than the OECD average (72%) and a lower share compared with all other neighbouring countries. The rest of health spending is paid mainly through direct out-of-pocket payments by patients (with private health insurances playing a very small role). The share of health spending paid directly by patients has increased significantly in Hungary since 2007, rising from 26% to 29% of overall health spending between 2007 and 2012, which is exactly 10 percentage points higher than the OECD average in 2012 (OECD/European Union, 2014). A growing share of direct out-of-pocket payments may create financial barriers to health care for certain population groups, particularly those with low income, unless some measures are taken to protect their access to care.

Access to health care

The Hungarian government has recently taken some measures to improve access to care, particularly for people living in rural areas, but there may be persistent issues related to financial access to care. Given the relatively low share of health spending that is publicly-funded, a greater share of household consumption is allocated to health spending, which may create access problems, particularly for people with low income. As already noted, in 2012, out-of-pocket payments were high compared to neighbouring countries and OECD countries. As a share of total household consumption, out-of-pocket medical spending reached 4.2% of final household consumption for the Hungarian population as a whole in 2012, compared with about 2.5% on average in CEEC countries (Figure 5.5). This share was much greater for certain segments of the population, notably people with below average income.

Figure 5.5. **Out-of-pocket medical spending as a share of final household consumption, Hungary, neighbouring countries and the EU average, 2012 (or nearest year)**

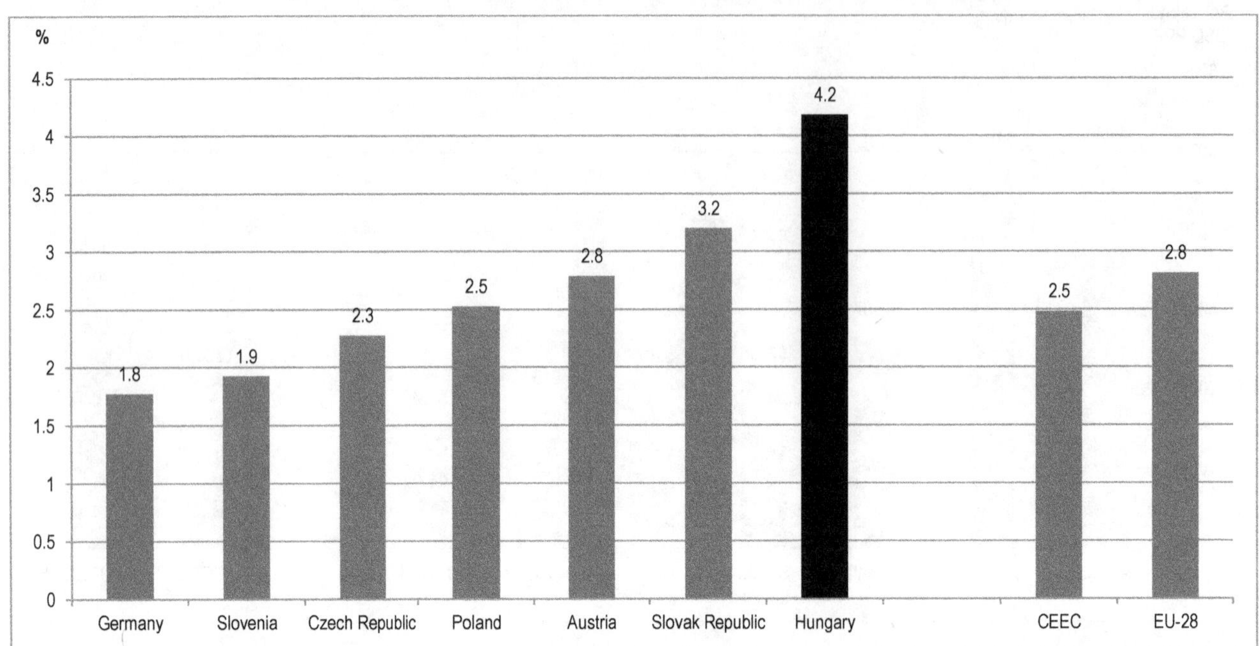

Source: OECD (2014a), *OECD Health Statistics* (database), http://dx.doi.org/10.1787/health-data-en (accessed on 21 March 2015).

StatLink http://dx.doi.org/10.1787/888933203010

According to the EU Survey of Income and Living Conditions (SILC), more than 15% of people with low income in Hungary reported having unmet care needs for medical examinations. This is more than three times higher than people in the highest income group, and among the highest proportion across all EU countries (Figure 5.6). These unmet care needs may be due not only to financial reasons, but also to geographic and other reasons.

As in other EU and OECD countries, there is an uneven distribution of doctors and health services across various geographic regions in Hungary. For example, in 2011, there were twice as many physicians working in urban areas than in rural areas in Hungary (Figure 5.7). In Hungary, as in other neighbouring countries such as the Slovak Republic and the Czech Republic, this wide gap is driven mainly by the strong concentration of physicians in the national capital region (Figure 5.8).

Between 2010 and 2012, the Hungarian government created outpatient units in 20 rural sub-regions that previously lacked capacities. These investments were funded by the EU Social Infrastructure Operative Programme and improved the access to specialist outpatient care for 430 000 people in Hungary (Elek, Varadi and Varga, 2013). Basic specialist outpatient care in the four main branches (internal medicine, surgery, obstetrics-gynaecology and paediatrics) can now be reached by about 310 000 more people in 20 minutes or less than before (according to recent estimates, at least 1.6 million people, or 16% of the population in Hungary, still live beyond this 20 minute limit).

Figure 5.6. **Unmet care needs for medical examinations by income level, Hungary, neighbouring countries and the EU average, 2012**

Note: Data for Austria are for 2011.

Source: Eurostat (2014), *Survey of Income and Living Conditions (SILC)* (database), http://ec.europa.eu/eurostat/web/microdata/european_union_statistics_on_income_and_living_conditions.

StatLink http://dx.doi.org/10.1787/888933203027

Figure 5.7. **Physician density in predominantly urban and rural regions (number of doctors per 1 000 population), Hungary and selected European countries, 2011 (or nearest year)**

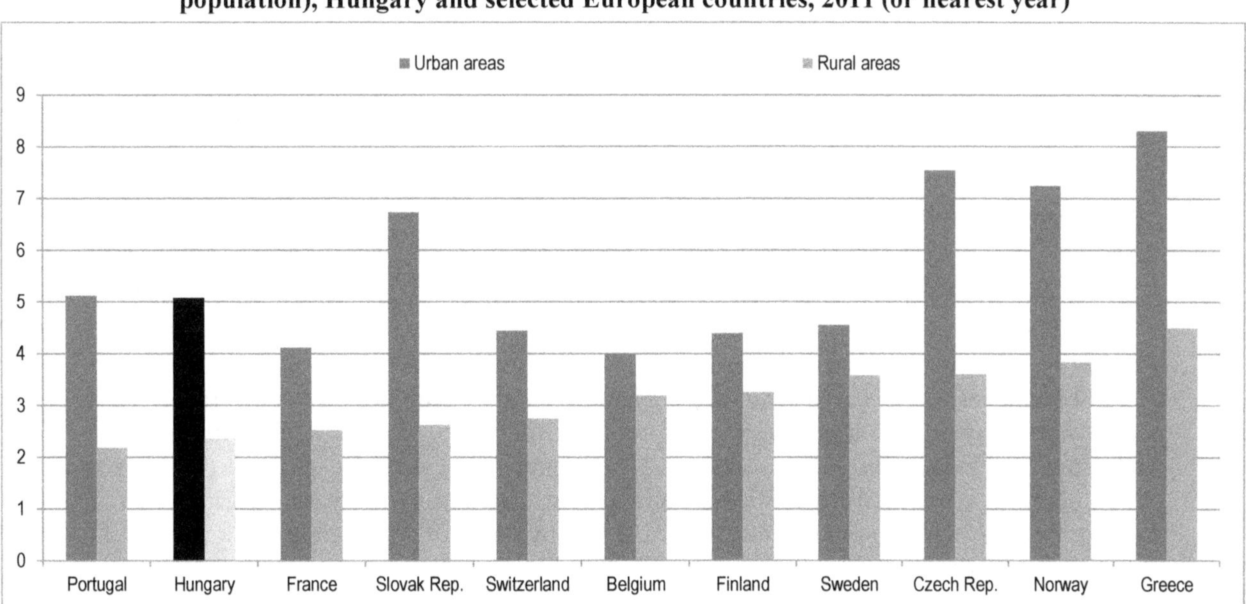

Note: Countries are ranked based on the number of doctors available in rural areas (lowest to highest).

Source: OECD (2013a), *OECD Regions at a Glance 2013*, OECD Publishing, Paris, http://dx.doi.org/10.1787/reg_glance-2013-en.

StatLink http://dx.doi.org/10.1787/888933203037

Figure 5.8. **Physician density by regions (number of doctors per 1000 population) in Hungary, 2011**

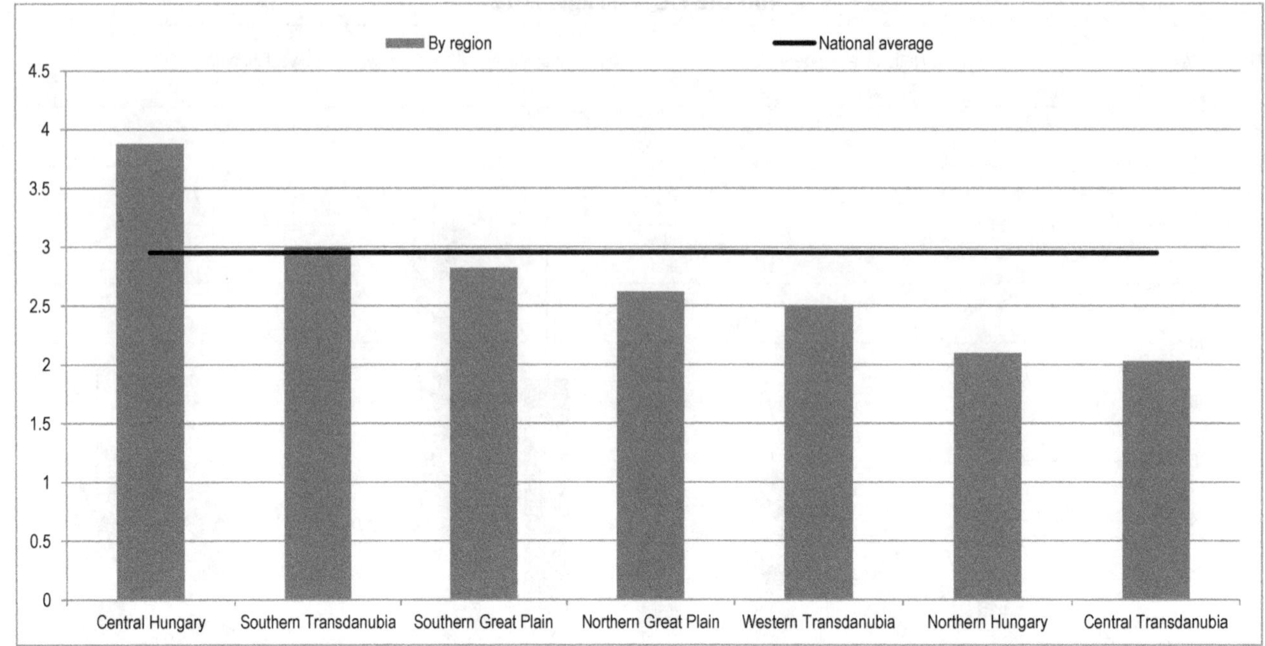

Source: OECD (2014b), *OECD Regional Statistics* (database), http://dx.doi.org/10.1787/region-data-en (accessed on 21 March 2015).

StatLink http://dx.doi.org/10.1787/888933203046

Efficiency and effectiveness of the health system

As in many other OECD countries, the health system in Hungary remains too "hospital centric", and a large share of spending (over one-third, 35%) is allocated to pharmaceuticals (compared with 20% on average across OECD countries), raising issues about the efficiency of this spending.

Regarding hospital care, the hospitalisation rate in Hungary is greater than in all other OECD countries, with the exception of Austria and Germany (Figure 5.9). Although the rate of avoidable hospital admissions (patients admitted to hospital for diseases that should usually be treated outside hospitals) has decreased in Hungary in recent years, it remains high compared to neighbouring countries and OECD countries, for health problems such as asthma and diabetes (OECD, 2013b).

Furthermore, the average length of stay of patients in hospital in Hungary is much greater than in most other OECD countries. In contrast to nearly all other European and OECD countries, the average length of stay in hospital in Hungary increased rather than decreased between 2007 and 2012 (Figure 5.10). On average, patients stayed for 9.5 days in hospital in Hungary in 2012, more than 25% longer than the OECD average (7.4 days). Looking more specifically at the length of stay for a normal delivery, Hungarian women stayed five days in hospital, compared with an average of only three days in OECD countries in 2012 (Figure 5.11).

Figure 5.9. **Hospital discharges for all conditions, Hungary, neighbouring countries and the OECD average, 2012**

Per 100 000 population

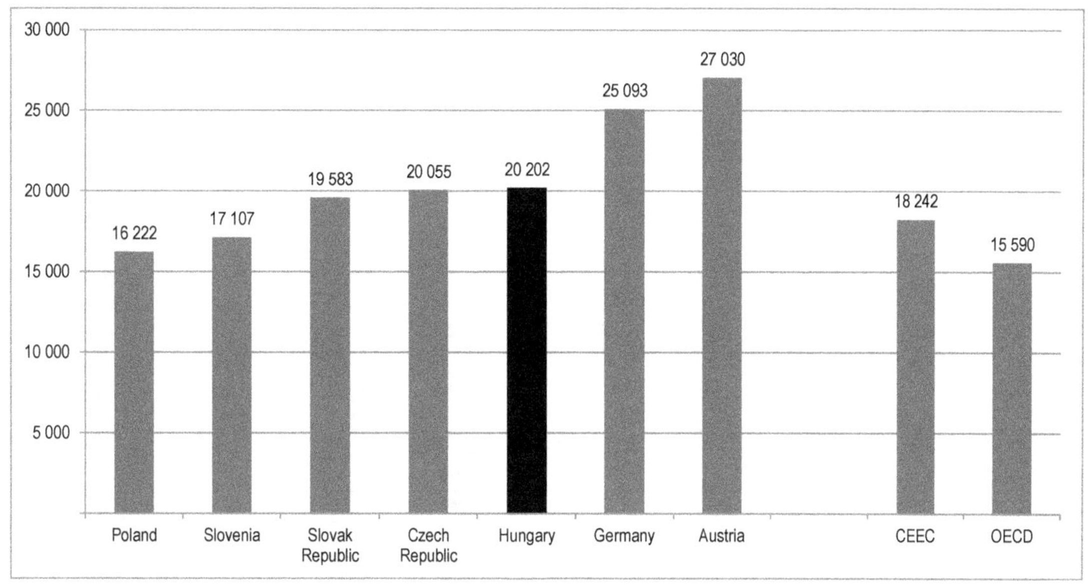

Source: OECD (2014a), *OECD Health Statistics* (database), http://dx.doi.org/10.1787/health-data-en (accessed on 21 March 2015).

StatLink http://dx.doi.org/10.1787/888933203053

Figure 5.10. **Average length of stay in hospital for all conditions, Hungary, neighbouring countries and the OECD average, 2007-12**

Number of days

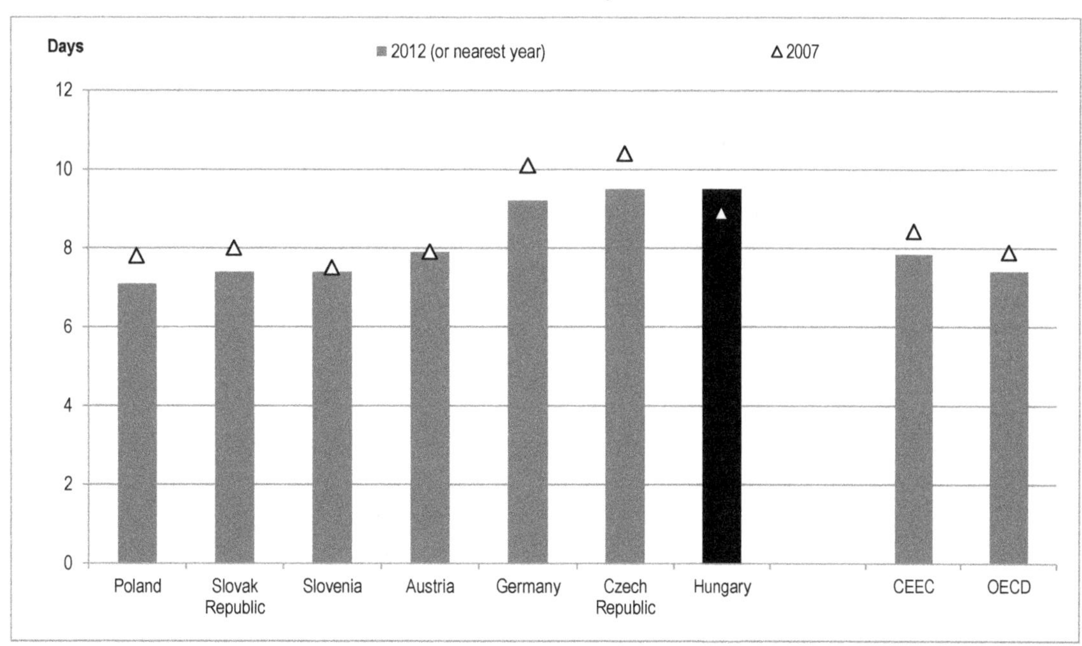

Source: OECD (2014a), *OECD Health Statistics* (database), http://dx.doi.org/10.1787/health-data-en (accessed on 21 March 2015).

StatLink http://dx.doi.org/10.1787/888933203068

Figure 5.11. **Average length of stay for normal delivery, Hungary, neighbouring countries and the OECD average, 2007-12**

Number of days

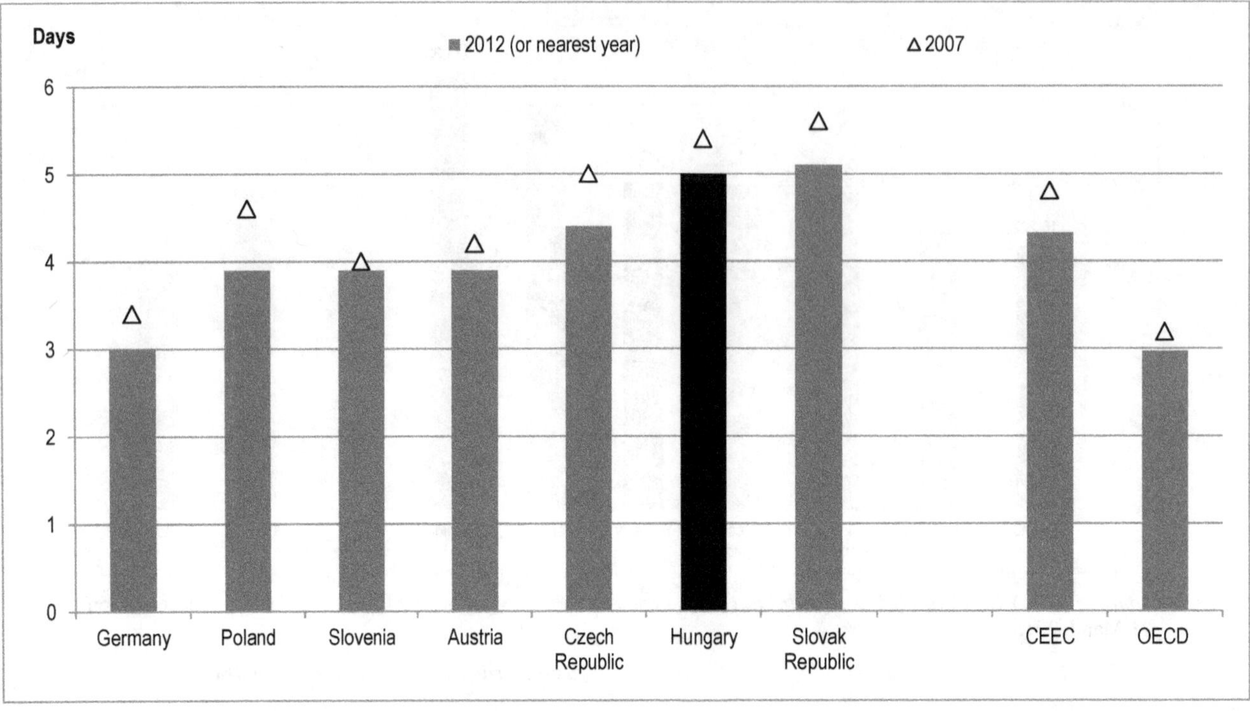

Source: OECD (2014a), *OECD Health Statistics* (database), http://dx.doi.org/10.1787/health-data-en (accessed on 21 March 2015).

StatLink http://dx.doi.org/10.1787/888933203076

The share of day surgery in Hungary (i.e. surgery which does not involve an overnight stay in hospital) remains much lower than in most other OECD countries. For example, while in most OECD countries, more than 80% of cataract operations are now performed as day surgery, this share remained below 40% in Hungary in 2012 (Figure 5.12). The share of day surgery for cataracts has increased in Hungary in recent years, but there is still room to achieve further efficiency gains.[1]

Figure 5.12. **Share of cataract surgeries carried out as day cases, Hungary, neighbouring countries and the OECD average, 2012**

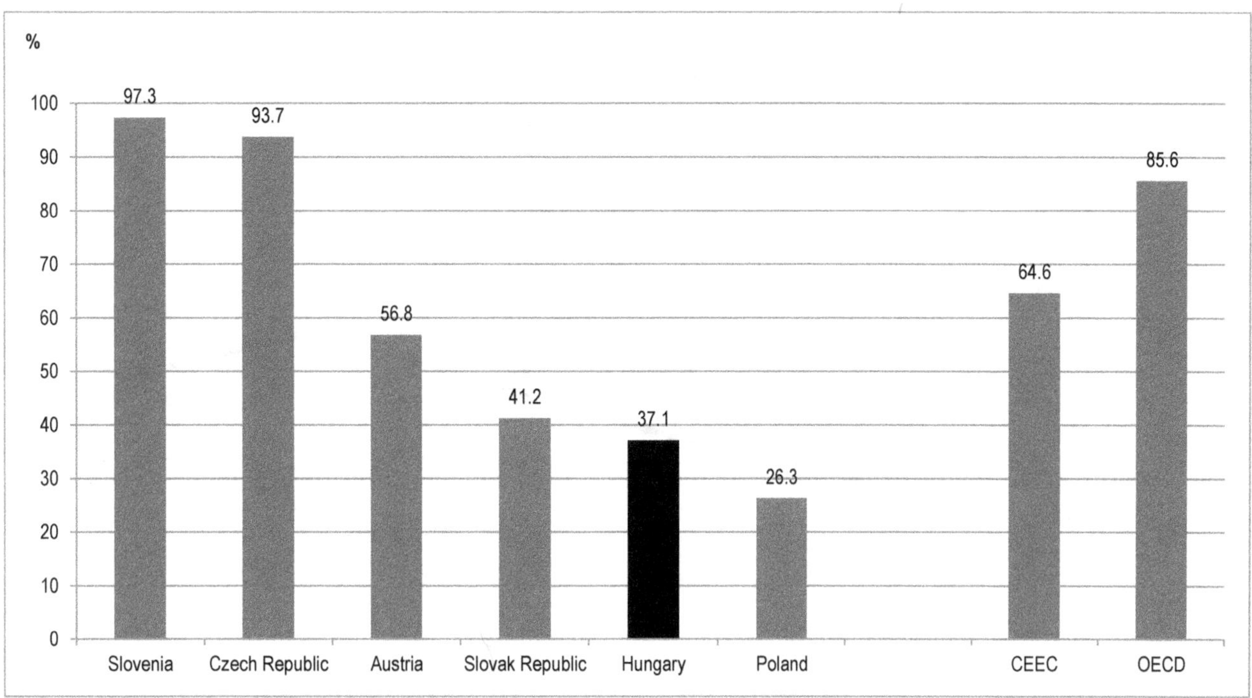

Source: OECD (2014a), *OECD Health Statistics* (database), http://dx.doi.org/10.1787/health-data-en (accessed on 21 March 2015).

StatLink http://dx.doi.org/10.1787/888933203087

Expenditure on pharmaceuticals

Even though total health spending in Hungary is only about half the OECD average, spending on pharmaceuticals is greater than the OECD average. This is because the share of health spending allocated to pharmaceuticals in Hungary is the highest among all OECD countries (along with the Slovak Republic), accounting for more than one-third of health spending.

As a percentage of GDP, expenditure on pharmaceuticals in Hungary is the highest among all OECD countries. In 2012, expenditure on pharmaceuticals accounted for 2.5% of GDP, which is more than 60% higher than the OECD average (1.5%). Of this 2.5%, less than half was financed by public funds while most of it was paid by private funds (mainly direct payments from patients).

On a per capita basis, expenditure on pharmaceuticals continued to increase in Hungary during the crisis, while it stagnated in many neighbouring and OECD countries (Figure 5.13). However, between 2011 and 2012, expenditure on pharmaceuticals has started to decrease by almost 7%. This is partly due to the expiry of patents for a number of "blockbuster" drugs which have led to substantial price reductions for new generics in Hungary, as in other countries, but also to the impact of the introduction of new mandatory tendering processes for publicly financed medications in Hungary, which has also resulted in significant price reductions. The distribution of some costly pharmaceuticals has also been shifted away from pharmacies to the hospital sector, so the spending is now included under hospital expenditure, thus over-estimating the real reduction in pharmaceutical spending.

Figure 5.13. **Total expenditure on pharmaceuticals and other medical non-durables, Hungary, neighbouring countries and the OECD average, 2007-12**

Per capita, USD purchasing power parity

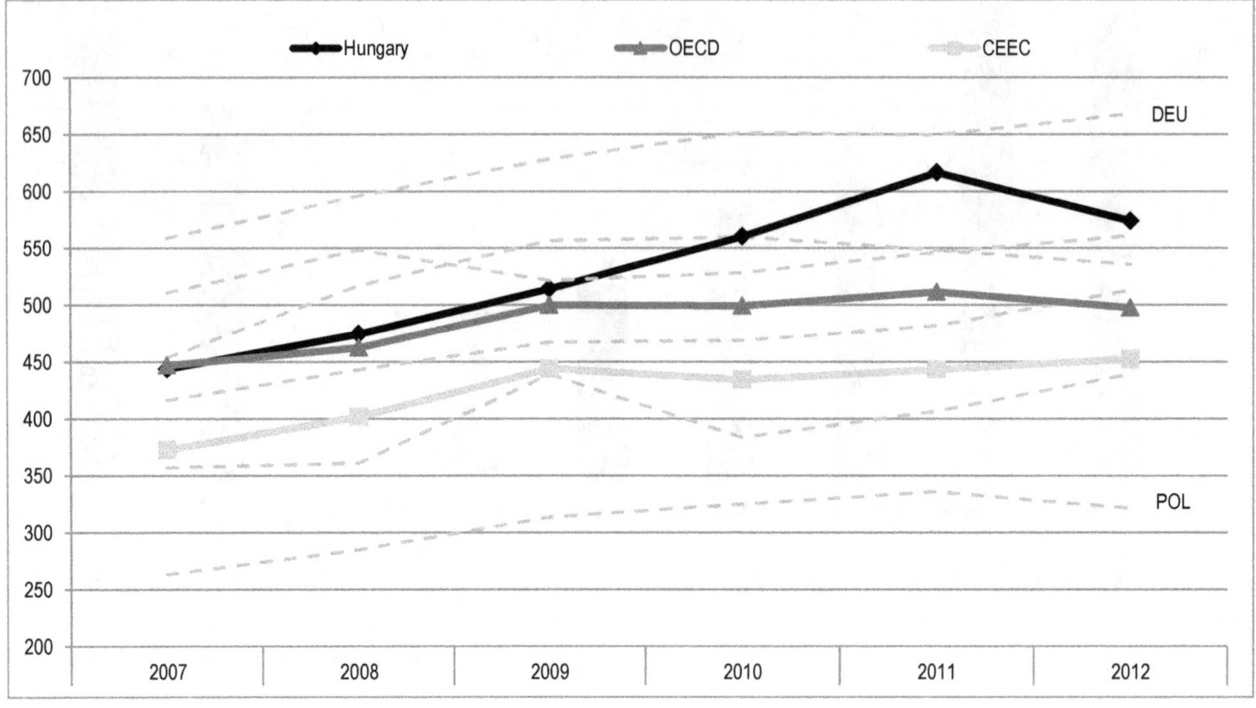

Source: OECD (2014a), *OECD Health Statistics* (database), http://dx.doi.org/10.1787/health-data-en (accessed on 21 March 2015).

StatLink http://dx.doi.org/10.1787/888933203095

The consumption of many categories of pharmaceutical drugs, including anti-hypertensive, anti-cholesterols and anti-diabetics, is greater in Hungary than in most of its neighbouring countries and the OECD average (OECD, 2013b), thus contributing to higher spending.

Further efforts will be needed to better manage both the prices and volumes of consumption of different types of pharmaceutical drugs in Hungary, in order to ensure greater value for the large amount of money spent on pharmaceuticals.

Notes

1. Cross-country comparisons should, however, be made with caution since the coverage of the data on same-day surgery varies across countries. For example, some countries such as the Czech Republic are able to report data on cataract surgery performed outside hospitals, while the data coverage in other countries, including Hungary, only includes activities in hospital.

Bibliography

Elek, Péter, Balazs Varadi and Marton Varga (2013), "Effects of geographical accessibility on the use of outpatient care services: Quasi-experimental evidence from Hungary", *Journal of Economic Literature*, JEL codes: I11, I18, C23, C25.

Eris, M. (2012), "Improving Health Outcomes and System in Hungary", *OECD Economics Department Working Papers*, No. 961, OECD Publishing, Paris, http://dx.doi.org/10.1787/5k98rwqj3zmp-en.

Eurostat (2014), *Survey of Income and Living Conditions (SILC)* (database), http://ec.europa.eu/eurostat/web/microdata/european_union_statistics_on_income_and_living_conditions.

OECD (2014a), *OECD Health Statistics* (database), http://dx.doi.org/10.1787/health-data-en (accessed on 21 March 2015).

OECD (2014b), *OECD Regional Statistics* (database), http://dx.doi.org/10.1787/region-data-en (accessed on 21 March 2015).

OECD (2013a), *OECD Regions at a Glance 2013*, OECD Publishing, Paris, http://dx.doi.org/10.1787/reg_glance-2013-en.

OECD (2013b), *Health at a Glance 2013: OECD Indicators*, OECD Publishing, Paris, http://dx.doi.org/10.1787/health_glance-2013-en.

OECD/European Union (2014), *Health at a Glance: Europe 2014*, OECD Publishing, Paris, http://dx.doi.org/10.1787/health_glance_eur-2014-en.

International surveys measuring confidence and satisfaction with government, institutions and services: Weblinks

Gallup World Poll: www.gallup.com.

Chapter 6

Government performance and the education system in Hungary

This chapter provides a set of indicators related to the performance of the education system in Hungary. It provides indicators on the general level of satisfaction of the population with education services, on the evolution of Hungary's Programme for International Student Assessment (PISA) scores since 2003 and on the evolution of public expenditure per student. It also provides indicators on learning outcomes by socio-economic background and on graduation rates from upper secondary school and tertiary education. Finally, it provides data on the education "premium" in terms of labour market outcome and salary levels in Hungary.

This chapter focusses on the performance of the education system in Hungary. Public satisfaction with the education system and schools has remained relatively low in Hungary. In 2013, public satisfaction fell below that of all Hungary's neighbouring countries and the OECD average. Public spending per student at the primary and secondary level is relatively low in Hungary, and has been decreasing between 2008 and 2011 as part of a broader austerity programme, while it increased in most its neighbouring countries and on average across OECD countries. The results of 15 year-old Hungarian students in the last round of the Programme for International Student Assessment (PISA) in 2012 have also been low compared with neighbouring countries, and have declined in mathematics over previous years. While the graduation rate from secondary education is among the highest across the OECD, tertiary education graduation remains relatively low in Hungary (although it has been steadily increasing in recent years). At the same time, attainment rates at the tertiary level are traditionally low, which can explain why there is a very large employment and income premium in obtaining a university degree in Hungary. Since its arrival in 2010, the new administration has undertaken major education system reforms that are currently being implemented. These reforms include a new Public Education Act, a new teachers' career path and centralisation of the financing and management of primary and secondary schools as part of the re-organisation of the territorial administration. These reforms might reduce inequalities of access across regions and improve the quality of education in Hungary in the coming years.

Citizen satisfaction with the education system and schools

Citizen satisfaction with the education system and schools has remained low in recent years in Hungary, decreasing slightly from 57% satisfaction in 2007 to 56% in 2013 according to a recent Gallup World Poll (Figure 6.1). This is below the rate of satisfaction in all neighbouring countries and across the OECD on average (67%). This low satisfaction rate with the education system is associated with low public spending on education per student and as a percentage of GDP.

Expenditure on education per student

Expenditure per student by educational institutions is largely influenced by teachers' salaries, pension systems, teaching hours, the cost of teaching material and facilities, the type of programmes provided (e.g. general or vocational) and the number of students enrolled in the education system (OECD, 2014).

In 2011 (latest year for which country data are available), annual expenditure on education per student – which only includes public institutions in Hungary, while it also includes private spending in some other countries - was generally lower in Hungary than in the Central and Eastern European countries (CEEC) and the OECD average, particularly for primary school and secondary school students. On average in Hungary in 2011, USD 4 566 adjusted for purchasing power parity (PPP) was spent per primary school student, USD 4 574 was spent per secondary school student and USD 9 209 was spent per university student (Figure 6.2). At primary and secondary schools, the spending gap between Hungary and the average across CEEC countries was 30% (48% with OECD average). The gap was smaller for tertiary education with Hungary spending only 2% less than the CEEC average (and 34% less than the OECD average).

Figure 6.1. **Citizens' satisfaction with the education system and schools, Hungary, neighbouring countries and the OECD average, 2007-13**

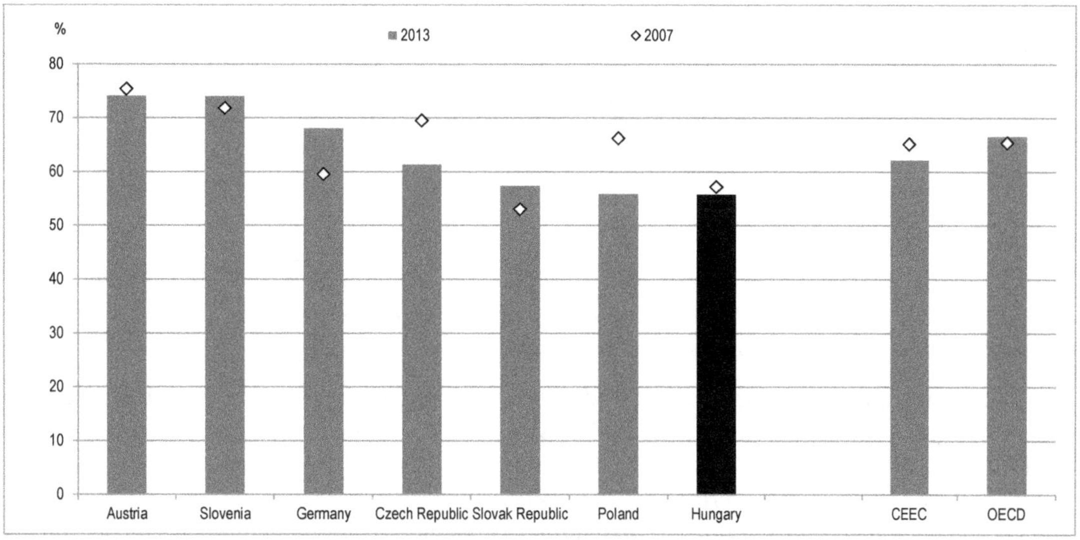

Note: Data for satisfaction with the education system and schools refer to the percentage of people responding that they were "satisfied" to the question, "In the city or area where you live, are you satisfied or dissatisfied with the educational system or the schools?" Data for Austria, the Slovak Republic and Slovenia are for 2006 rather than 2007.

Source: Gallup World Poll, www.gallup.com.

StatLink http://dx.doi.org/10.1787/888933203107

Figure 6.2. **Annual expenditure per student by level of education, Hungary, neighbouring countries and the OECD average, 2011**

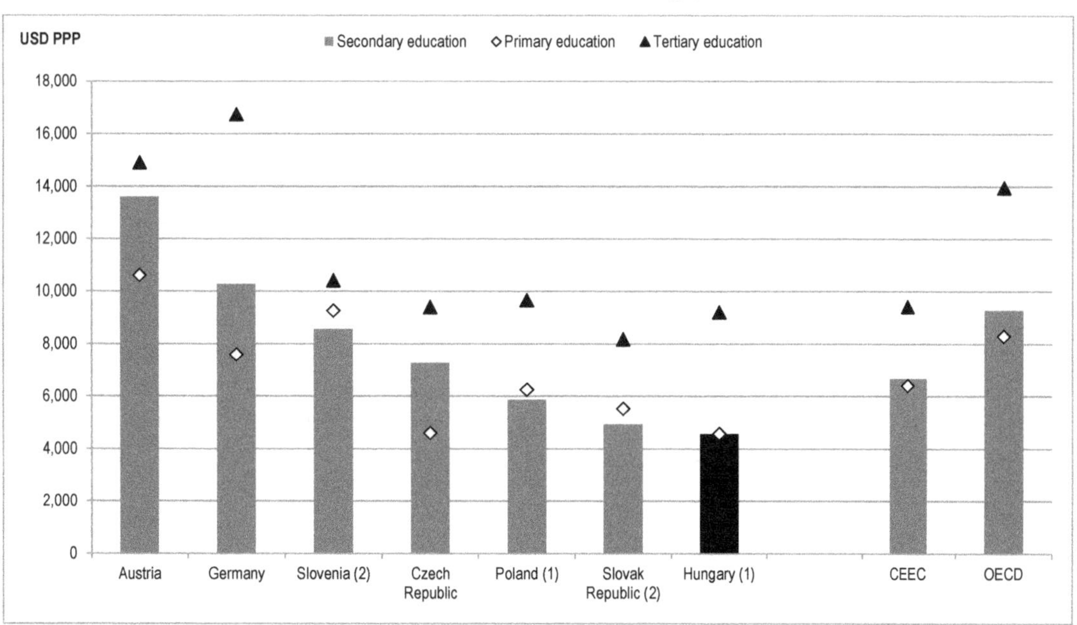

1. Public institutions only.
2. Some levels of education are included with others.

Source: OECD (2014), *Education at a Glance 2014: OECD Indicators*, OECD Publishing, Paris, http://dx.doi.org/10.1787/eag-2014-en.

StatLink http://dx.doi.org/10.1787/888933203113

Between 2008 and 2011, spending per student in primary, secondary and post-secondary (non-tertiary) education decreased by 14 percentage points in real terms in Hungary, while it increased by 13 percentage points in CEEC countries, and by more than 5 percentage points in OECD countries, on average (Figure 6.3). On the other hand, spending on tertiary education increased significantly between 2008 and 2011 in Hungary (+13 percentage points), but this is due partly to a reduction in the number of students registered in public universities (-7 percentage points).

Progress in PISA results since 2000

In the 2012 PISA cycle, Hungarian students scored, on average, 477 in mathematics, 494 in science and 488 in reading, which is generally below the other CEEC countries (except the Slovak Republic) and the OECD average (Figure 6.4).

Focussing only on mathematics, the score of Hungarian students has decreased by 1.3 points per year on average since 2003, while the decrease has been more moderate in CEEC countries (-0.5 points) and OECD countries (-0.3 points) on average (Figure 6.5). The scores of Poland and Germany for instance have significantly increased during that period (+2.6 points and 1.4 points, respectively). Poland's good results can be attributed to two sets of reforms in the late 1990s and in 2009 that modified the structure of the education system and provided teachers with more flexibility to adapt the national curriculum to their students in primary and lower secondary school (as long as it remained aligned with the national framework).

Hungary has traditionally been characterised by significant gaps in PISA performance, depending on school location. The gap between the average score of students in mathematics in 2012 in rural areas and large cities (cities with more than 100 000 inhabitants) was significantly higher in Hungary (54 points) than across the OECD on average (34 points). Analysis of the 2012 PISA results also shows that the between-school variation in mathematics score in Hungary is higher (63%) than the within-school variation (39%), while on average in CEEC and OECD countries the within-school variation is higher than between-school variation (OECD, 2013b).

There are also persistent education performance gaps with regard to the socio-economic background of students. While on average in OECD countries, 15% of the variation in student performance in mathematics can be explained by differences in their socio-economic status, this percentage is much higher in Hungary, reaching 23% in 2012 (Figure 6.6). Although this percentage has slightly decreased since 2003 (-3 percentage points), disadvantaged students are still less likely to achieve high levels of performance (and therefore weight relatively more negatively in the country's mean score). Further efforts might therefore be required to provide greater support to reduce the gaps in student performance between students of lower and higher socio-economic backgrounds.

Figure 6.3. **Change in expenditure per student by educational institutions, Hungary, neighbouring countries and the OECD average, 2008-11**

Index of change between 2008 and 2011 (2008 = 100, 2011 constant prices)

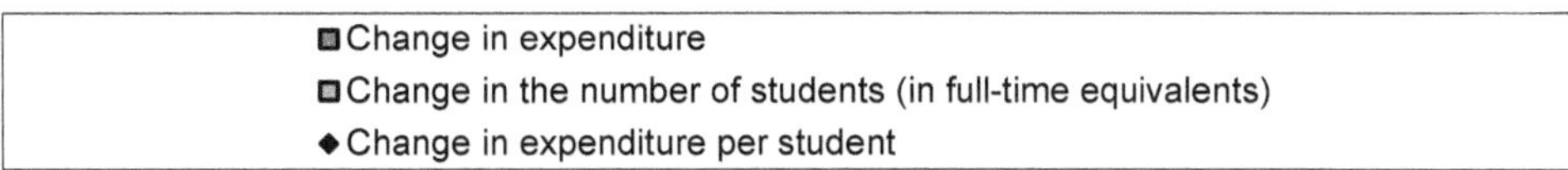

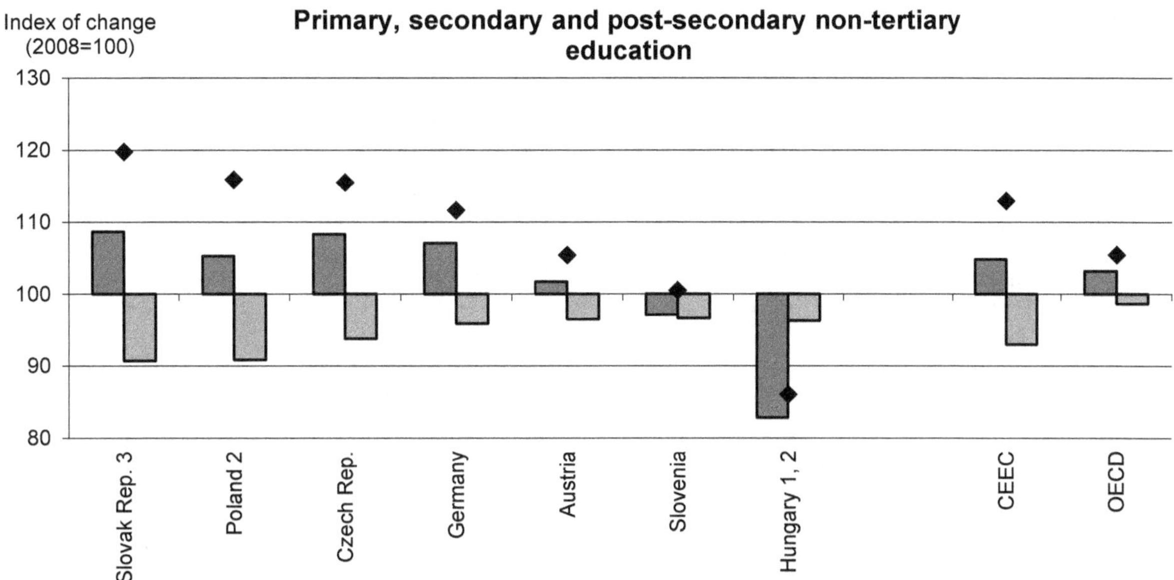

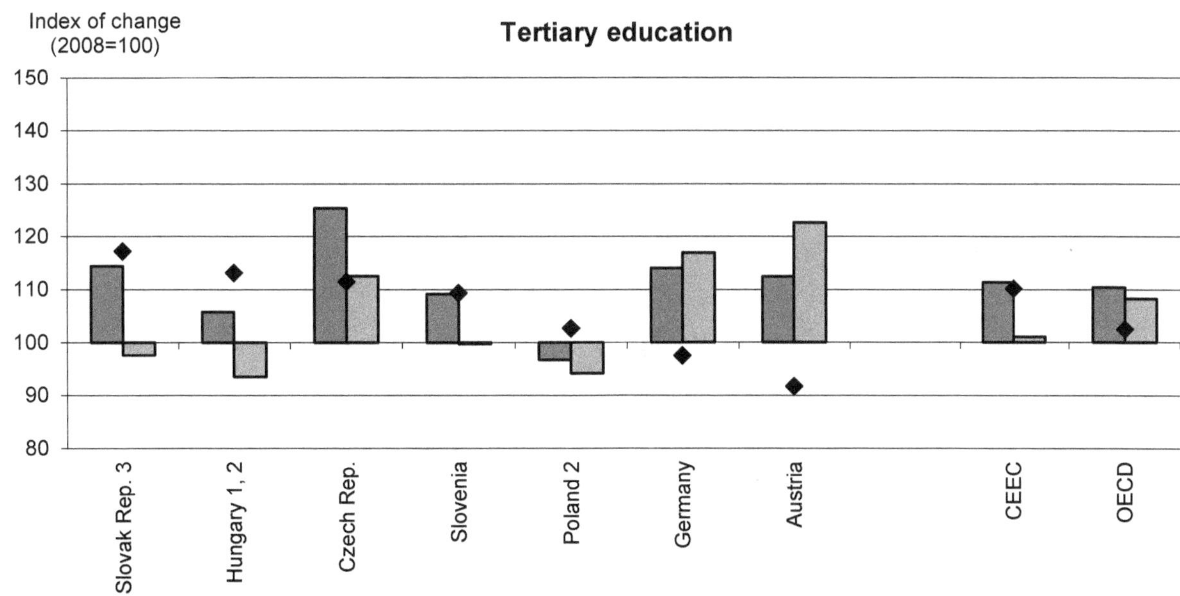

1. Public expenditure only.
2. Public institutions only.
3. Some levels of education are included with others.
Countries are ranked in descending order of change in expenditure per student by educational institutions.
Source: OECD (2014), *Education at a Glance 2014: OECD Indicators*, OECD Publishing, Paris, http://dx.doi.org/10.1787/eag-2014-en.

StatLink http://dx.doi.org/10.1787/888933203126

Figure 6.4. **PISA scores in mathematics, science and reading, Hungary, neighbouring countries and the OECD average, 2012**

	Mathematics	Reading	Science
Poland	518	518	526
Germany	514	508	524
Austria	506	490	506
Czech Republic	499	493	508
Slovenia	501	481	514
Hungary	477	488	494
Slovak Republic	482	463	471
CEEC	500	489	505
OECD	494	496	501

Note: Countries are ranked in descending order of their mean score in PISA.

Source: OECD (2013a), "PISA: Programme for International Student Assessment", *OECD Education Statistics* (database), http://dx.doi.org/10.1787/data-00365-en (accessed on 21 March 2015).

StatLink http://dx.doi.org/10.1787/888933203136

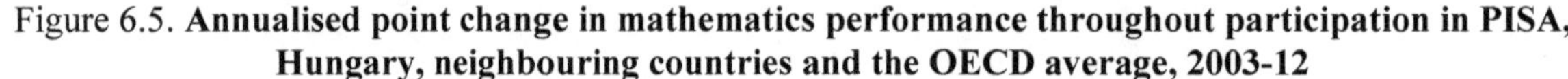

Figure 6.5. **Annualised point change in mathematics performance throughout participation in PISA, Hungary, neighbouring countries and the OECD average, 2003-12**

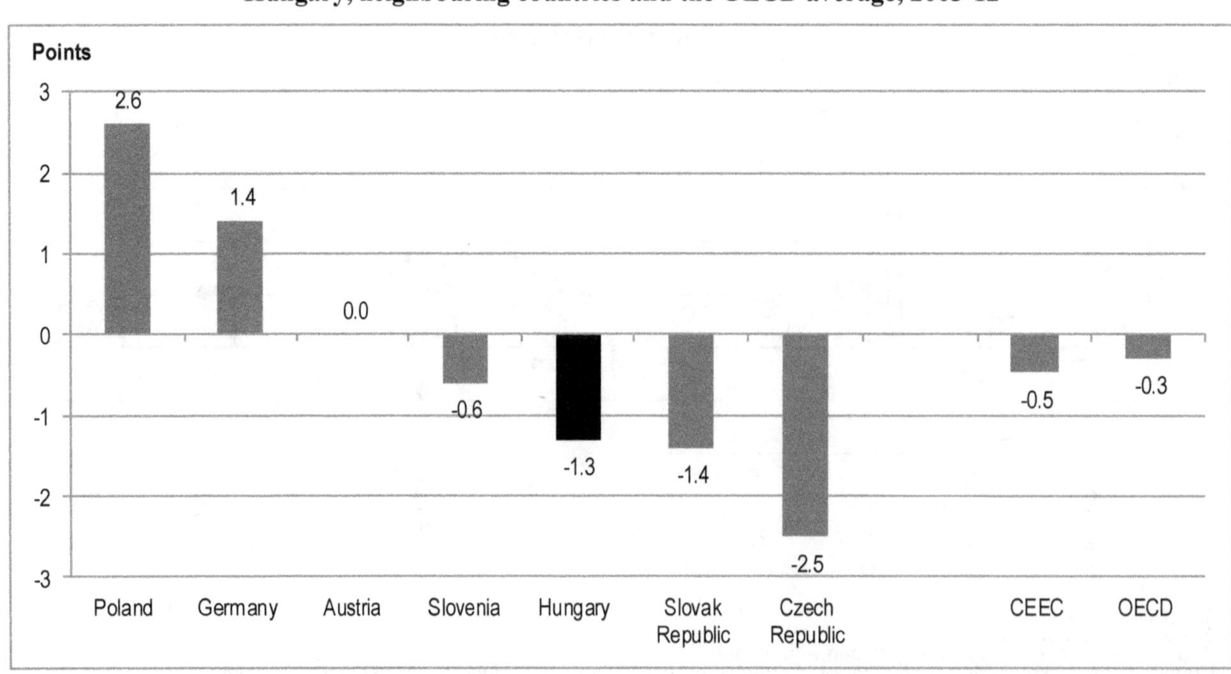

Source: OECD (2014), *Education at a Glance 2014: OECD Indicators*, OECD Publishing, Paris, http://dx.doi.org/10.1787/eag-2014-en.

StatLink http://dx.doi.org/10.1787/888933203146

Figure 6.6. **Relationship between performance in mathematics and socio-economic status, Hungary, neighbouring countries and the OECD average, 2003 and 2012**

Percentage of explained variance in mathematics performance

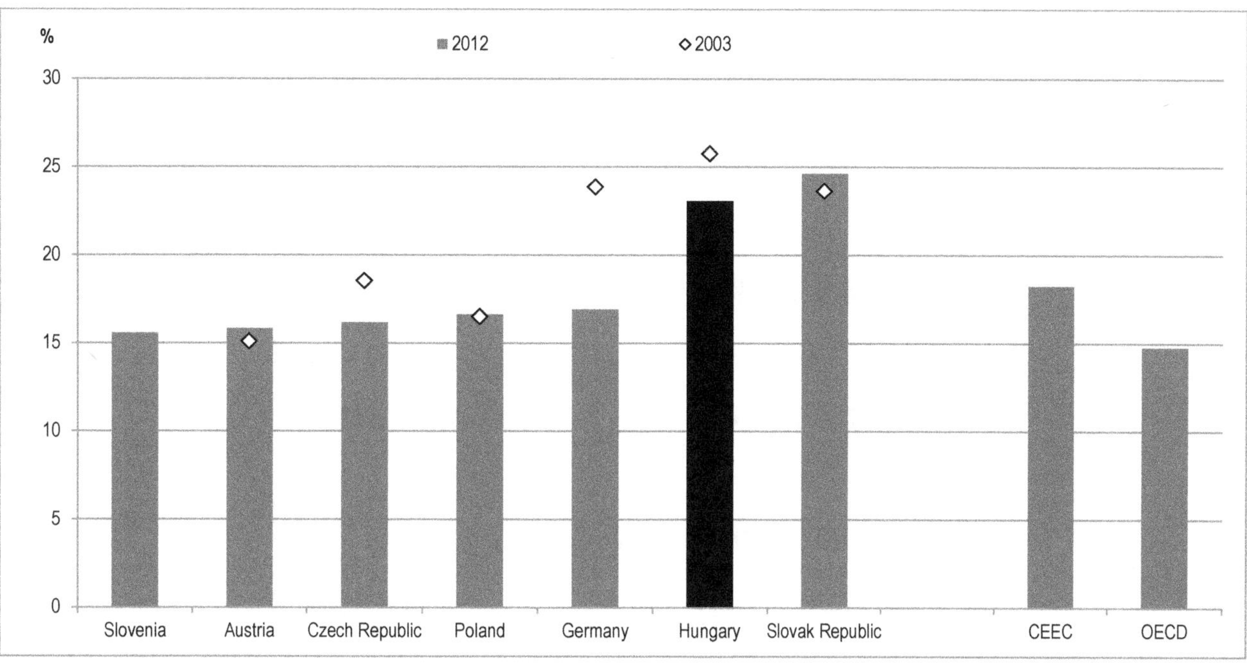

Note: The results are based on students' self-reports and single-level bivariate regression of performance on the Economic, Social and Cultural Status (ESCS).

Source: OECD (2014), *Education at a Glance 2014: OECD Indicators*, OECD Publishing, Paris, http://dx.doi.org/10.1787/eag-2014-en.

StatLink http://dx.doi.org/10.1787/888933203151

Teachers' salaries

Beyond improving access to good education for disadvantaged groups, it is also crucial to ensure a high-quality and highly motivated teaching staff in primary and secondary schools across Hungary. Given that teachers' salaries are the single largest cost in education, the setting of their salary level is a critical consideration for policy makers seeking to ensure both the quality of teaching and a sustainable education budget.

In 2012, the average salary of a primary school teacher with 15 years of experience and minimum training in Hungary was 35% lower than in other CEEC countries and 65% lower than the OECD average (adjusted for purchasing power parity). Regarding upper secondary teachers, their statutory salary after ten years of experience and minimum training was 310% lower than the average in other CEEC countries and 654% lower than the OECD average (OECD, 2014).

Compared to the average earnings of all tertiary educated workers, primary school teachers earn only slightly more than half of people with a tertiary education degree, and upper secondary school teachers about 60% of their salary. This is well below the CEEC average (about 65% for both primary and secondary school teachers) and the OECD average (85% and 92%, respectively) (Figure 6.7).

Figure 6.7. **Teachers' salaries for 25-64 year-olds relative to earnings for full-time, full-year workers with tertiary education, Hungary, neighbouring countries and the OECD average, 2012**

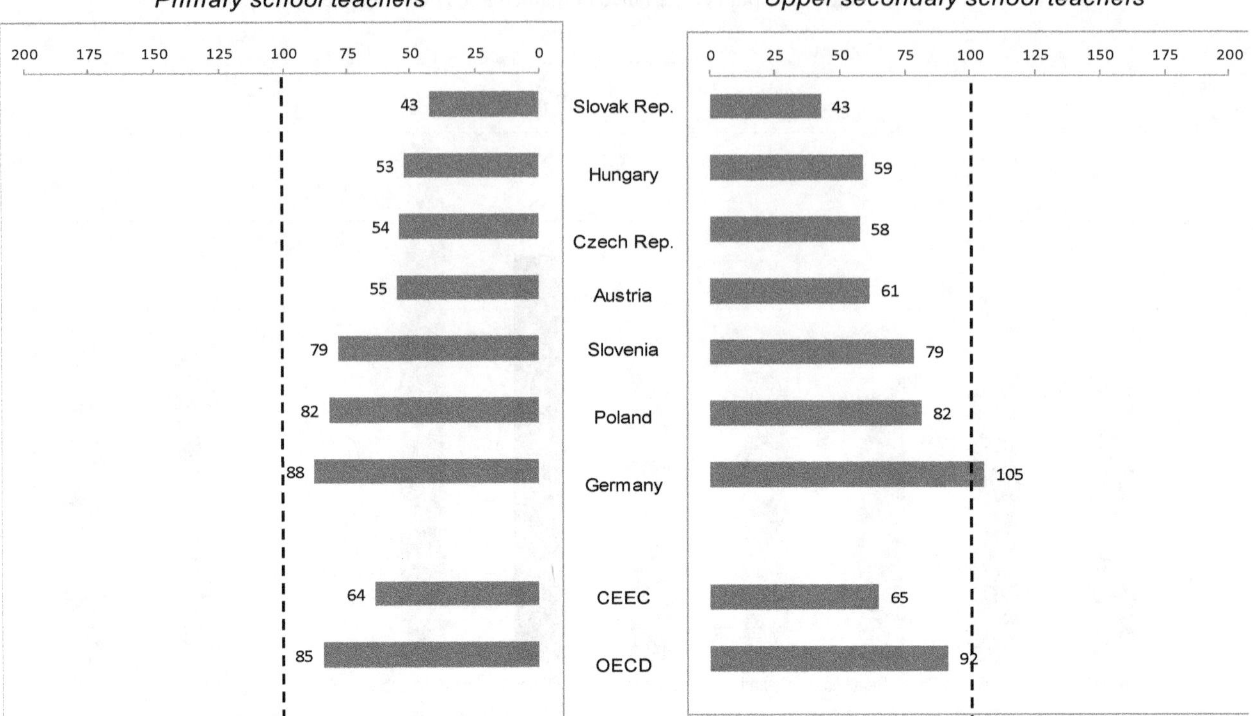

Source: OECD (2014), *Education at a Glance 2014: OECD Indicators*, OECD Publishing, Paris, http://dx.doi.org/10.1787/eag-2014-en.

StatLink http://dx.doi.org/10.1787/888933203169

Primary school teachers' salaries in Hungary fell in real terms by almost 30% between 2005 and 2012, while the salary of upper secondary teachers fell by nearly 35% over the same period (Figures 6.8 and 6.9). Between 2011 and 2012, teachers' salaries continued to decrease by 4.3% for primary school teachers and 5.6% for upper secondary school teachers. Hungary is the only CEEC country with available time series data where teachers' salaries in primary and secondary schools are lower in 2012 compared to 2005. The Hungarian government took a series of measures in 2013 and 2014 to improve the working conditions of teachers, including a 34% salary increase on average for 150 000 teachers starting in 2013 and further hikes every year until 2017, with the aim of closing the gap with the CEEC average in coming years.

Figure 6.8. **Evolution of primary school teachers' salaries (2005 = base 100), Hungary, neighbouring countries and the OECD average, 2005-12**

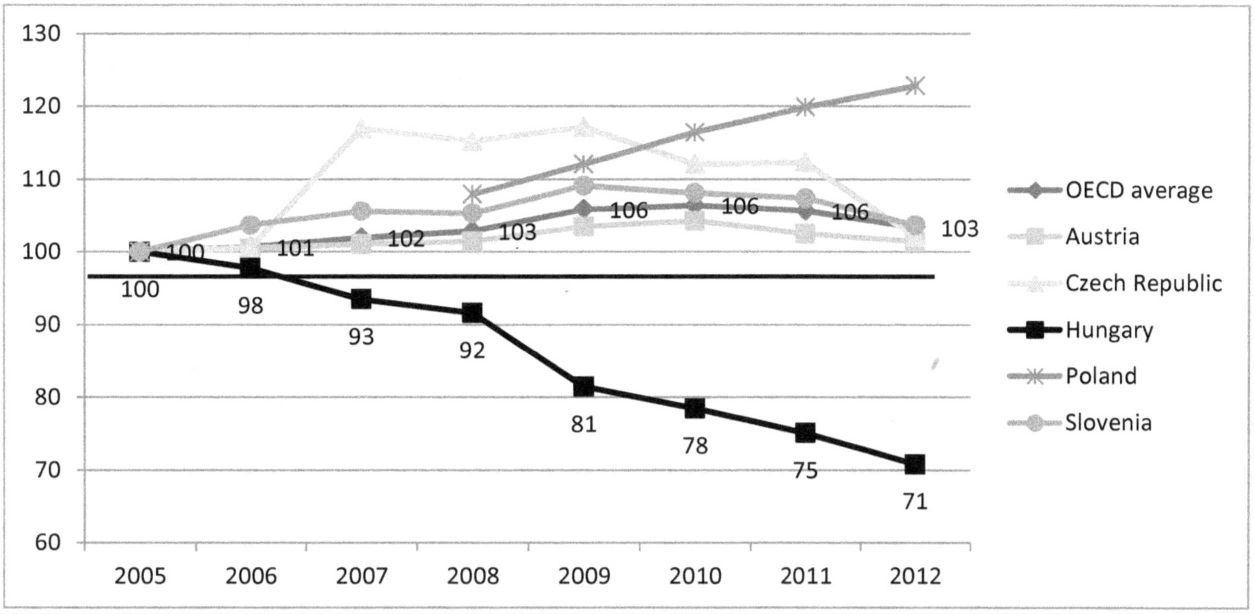

Source: OECD (2014), *Education at a Glance 2014: OECD Indicators*, OECD Publishing, Paris, http://dx.doi.org/10.1787/eag-2014-en.

StatLink http://dx.doi.org/10.1787/888933203174

Figure 6.9. **Evolution of upper secondary school teachers' salaries (2005 = base 100), Hungary, neighbouring countries and the OECD average, 2005-12**

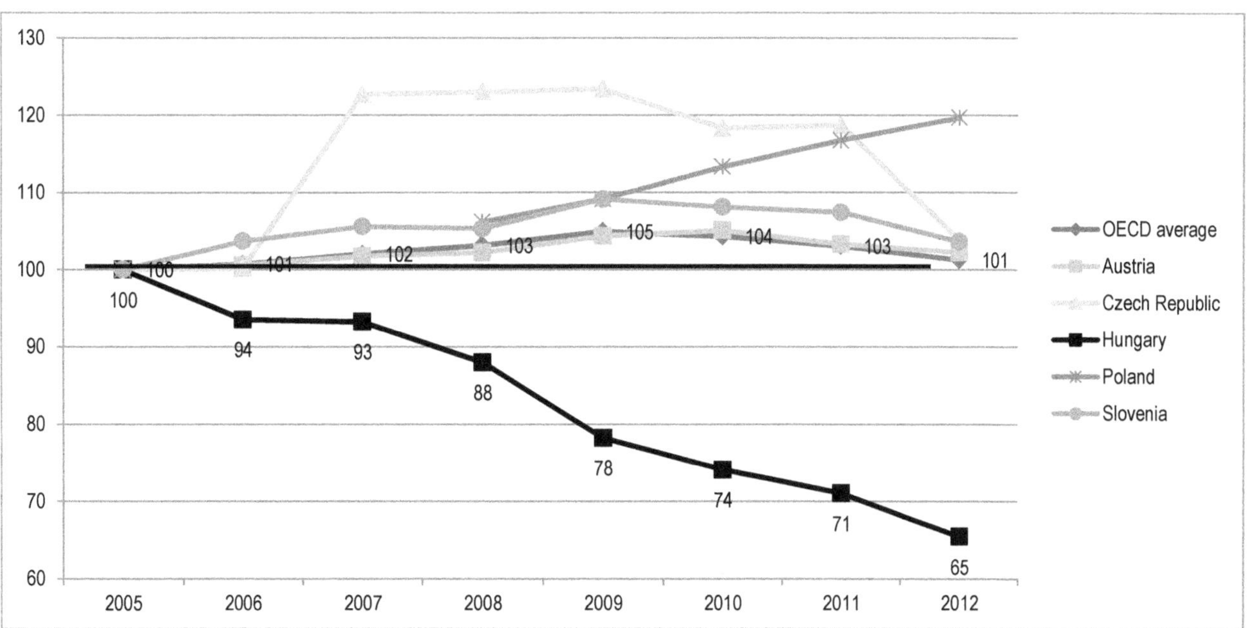

Source: OECD (2014), *Education at a Glance 2014: OECD Indicators*, OECD Publishing, Paris, http://dx.doi.org/10.1787/eag-2014-en.

StatLink http://dx.doi.org/10.1787/888933203184

Upper secondary and tertiary graduation rates

For many years, graduation rates from upper secondary school have been much higher in Hungary than in other CEEC countries, and even higher than in other OECD countries. In 2012 in Hungary, 94% of young people were expected to graduate from upper secondary school during their lifetime, which is above the CEEC average (87%) and the OECD average (84%) (Figure 6.10).

Figure 6.10. **Upper secondary graduation rate, Hungary, neighbouring countries and the OECD average, 2012**

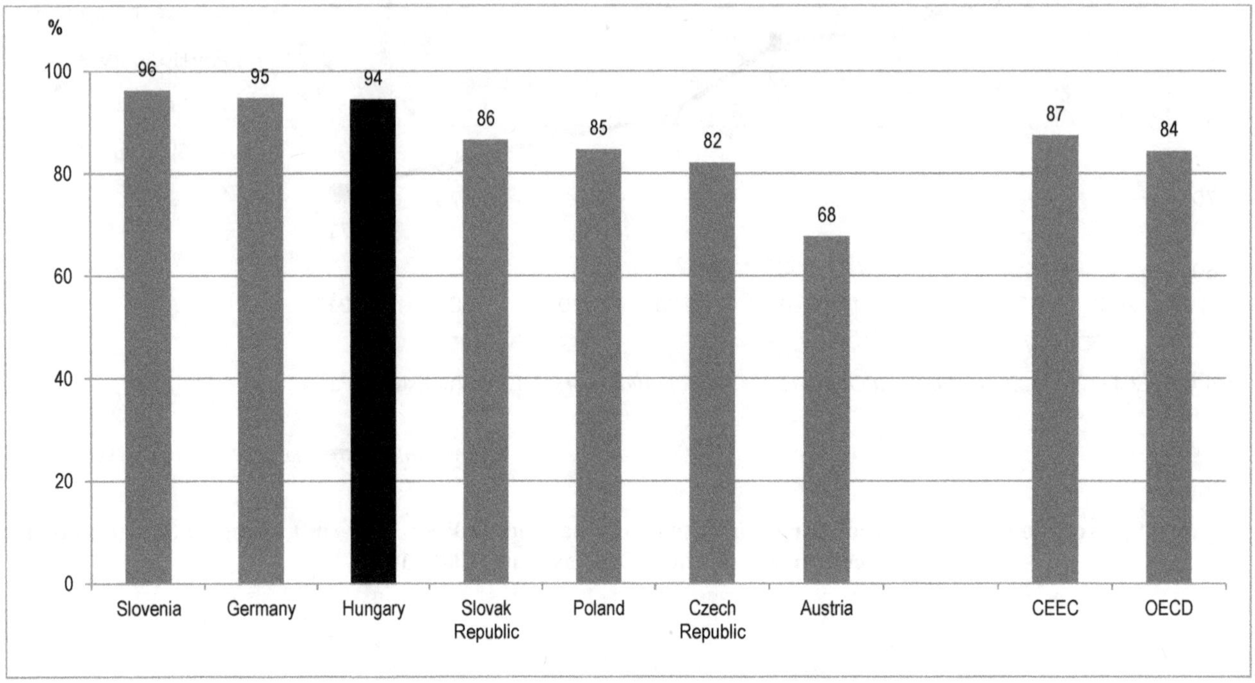

Note: For Austria, programmes spanning ISCED levels 3 and 4 (*Höhere berufsbildende Schule*) are not included.

Source: OECD (2014), *Education at a Glance 2014: OECD Indicators*, OECD Publishing, Paris, http://dx.doi.org/10.1787/eag-2014-en.

StatLink http://dx.doi.org/10.1787/888933203196

On the other hand, only about 23% of young people are expected to graduate from tertiary type A education (academic programmes) and 8% from tertiary type B education (vocational programmes) (Figure 6.11). This is well below all Hungary's neighbouring countries and the OECD average (37% for tertiary type A and 11% for tertiary type B). Moreover, this graduation rate from tertiary education programmes in Hungary has considerably decreased since 2010; this is associated with a significant increase in tuition fees (OECD, 2014). Given that the rate of young people entering tertiary type A has been relatively stable over the past few years, this suggests that the main challenge in increasing educational attainment in Hungary is to retain students and support them in finishing their tertiary education programmes.

Figure 6.11. **Graduation rate in tertiary education, Hungary, neighbouring countries and the OECD average, 2012**

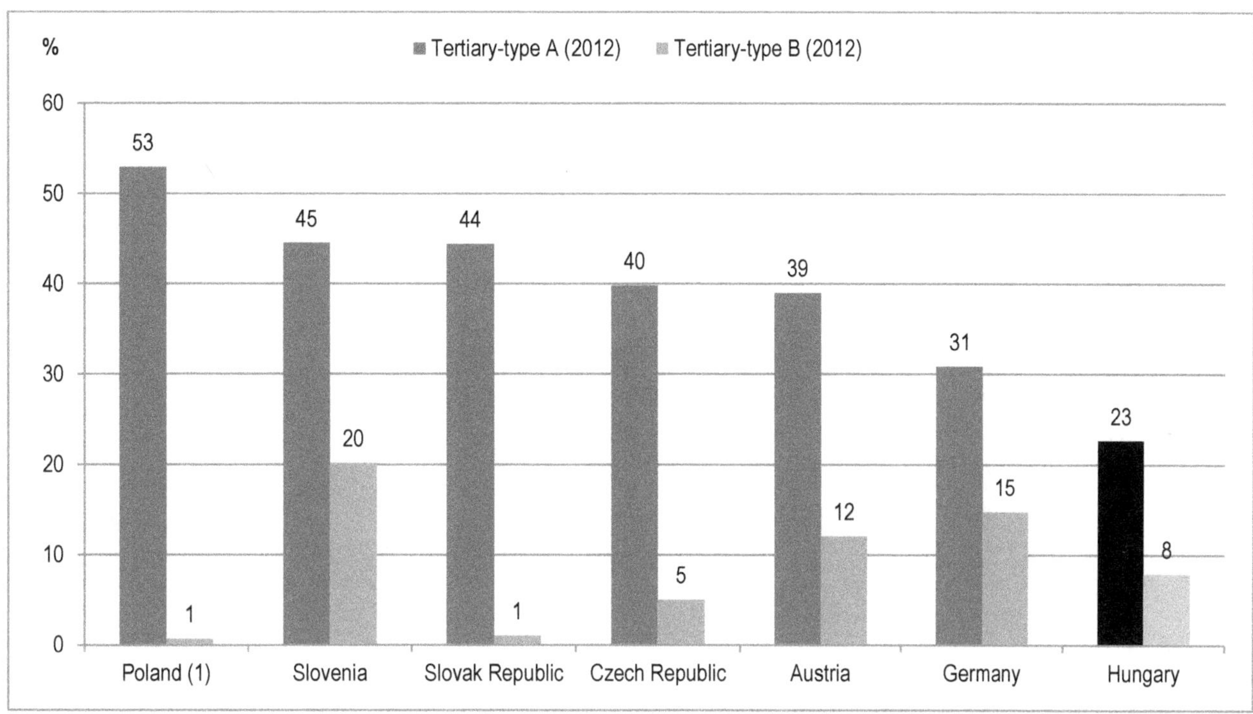

Source: OECD (2014), *Education at a Glance 2014: OECD Indicators*, OECD Publishing, Paris, http://dx.doi.org/10.1787/eag-2014-en.

StatLink http://dx.doi.org/10.1787/888933203206

Public subsidies to support tertiary students remain lower in Hungary than in most neighbouring countries and OECD countries. In 2011, the share of public expenditure on tertiary education dedicated to scholarships or other grants was only 12.4%, which is much lower than the share allocated in OECD countries (22.8%), which also includes student loans and transfers and payments to other private entities (Figure 6.12). Although more robust data on tuition fees and cost of studies would be needed to allow for more accurate cross-country comparison, this suggests that there might be scope to further support more university students in finishing their degrees.

Figure 6.12. **Public support for education to households and other private entities as a percentage of total public expenditure on tertiary education, Hungary, neighbouring countries and the OECD average, 2011**

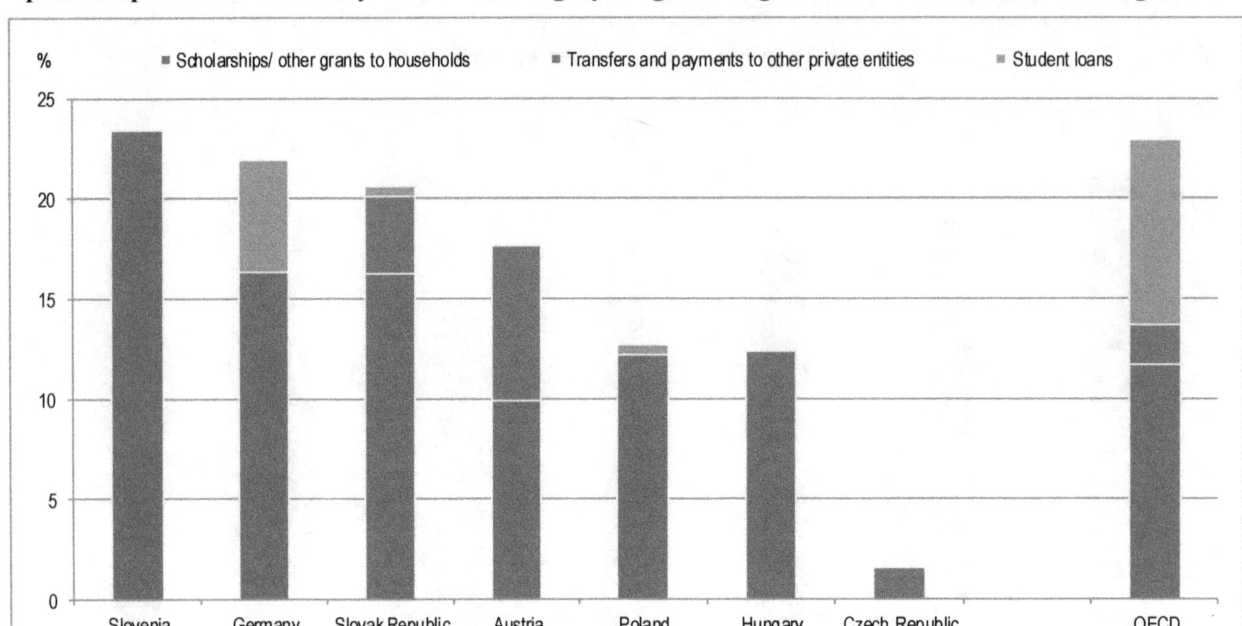

Source: OECD (2014), *Education at a Glance 2014: OECD Indicators*, OECD Publishing, Paris, http://dx.doi.org/10.1787/eag-2014-en.

StatLink http://dx.doi.org/10.1787/888933203213

Employment and earning "premium" of tertiary education

Higher educational achievements benefit both individuals and society, not only financially but in well-being, in areas such as better health outcomes and more civically engaged societies. It is also a determinant factor in ensuring labour productivity growth and competitiveness in an economy.

In Hungary, among those who graduate with a university degree, the premium in terms of employment opportunities and earning gains is large (compared with those who have only a secondary degree). In 2012, the unemployment rate of tertiary educated youth (aged 25-34 years old) was four times lower (5.7%) than the unemployment rate of youth with below upper secondary education (27.9%) and two times below the unemployment rate of youth who had completed upper secondary education (12.7%) (Figure 6.13). The unemployment rate of youth with a university degree in Hungary in 2012 was lower than the CEEC average (8.0%) and the OECD average (7.5%).

Figure 6.13. **Unemployment rate of youth by level of education, Hungary, neighbouring countries and the OECD average, 2012**

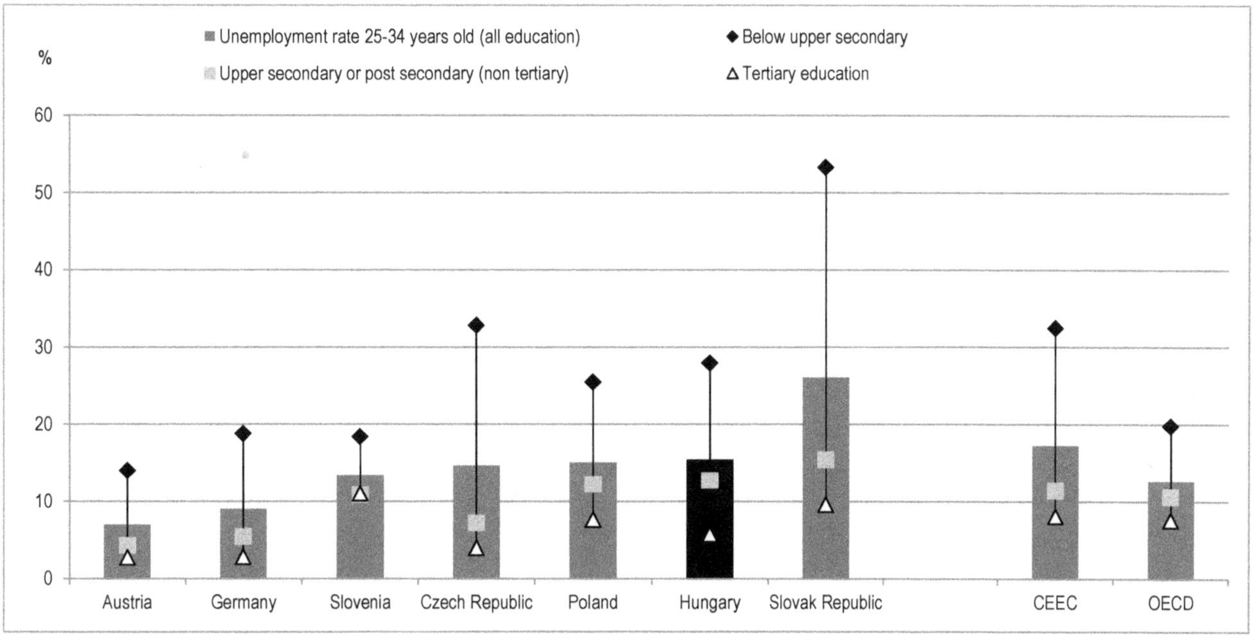

Notes: Data for below upper secondary education in Slovenia refer to 2011, rather than 2012.

Source: OECD (2014), *Education at a Glance 2014: OECD Indicators*, OECD Publishing, Paris, http://dx.doi.org/10.1787/eag-2014-en.

StatLink http://dx.doi.org/10.1787/888933203225

Between 2007 and 2012, tertiary educated youth were relatively more "protected" from unemployment than youth with below upper secondary education. The unemployment rate of tertiary educated youth increased by 2.5 percentage points between 2007 and 2012, while it increased by 5.5 percentage points for youth with below upper secondary education (reaching a peak of 32.6% in 2010) (Figure 6.14).

Figure 6.14. **Evolution of the unemployment rate of youth, by level of education, in Hungary, 2000-12**

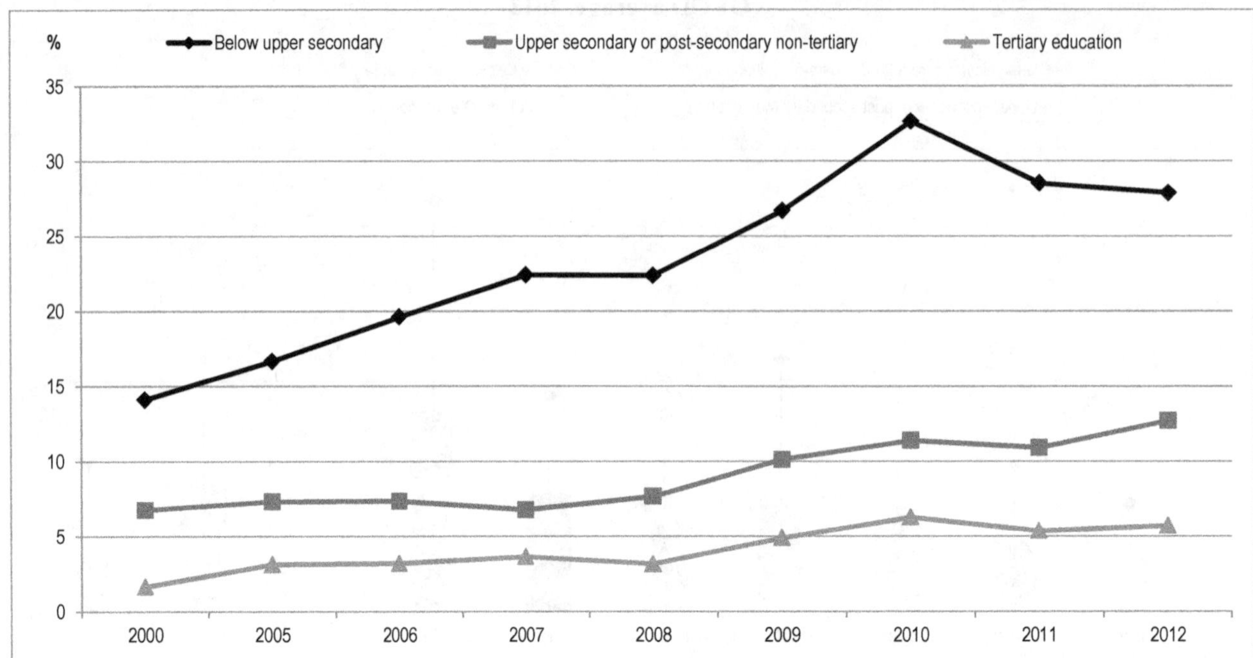

Source: OECD (2014), *Education at a Glance 2014: OECD Indicators*, OECD Publishing, Paris, http://dx.doi.org/10.1787/eag-2014-en.

StatLink http://dx.doi.org/10.1787/888933203237

In addition, tertiary educated people in Hungary in 2012 earned on average more than twice the average salary of those who had only completed secondary education, and an even greater difference compared to those who had not completed their secondary education. This earning gap is greater than the gap in CEEC countries and the OECD average (Figure 6.15). There remains, however, a significant gender gap in the levels of earnings of tertiary educated people in Hungary (about 60 percentage points' gap in earnings on average between men and women), which also exists in many neighbouring countries.

Figure 6.15. **Relative earnings of workers, by educational attainment and gender, Hungary, neighbouring countries and the OECD average, 2012**

25-64 year-olds with income from employment; upper secondary education = 100

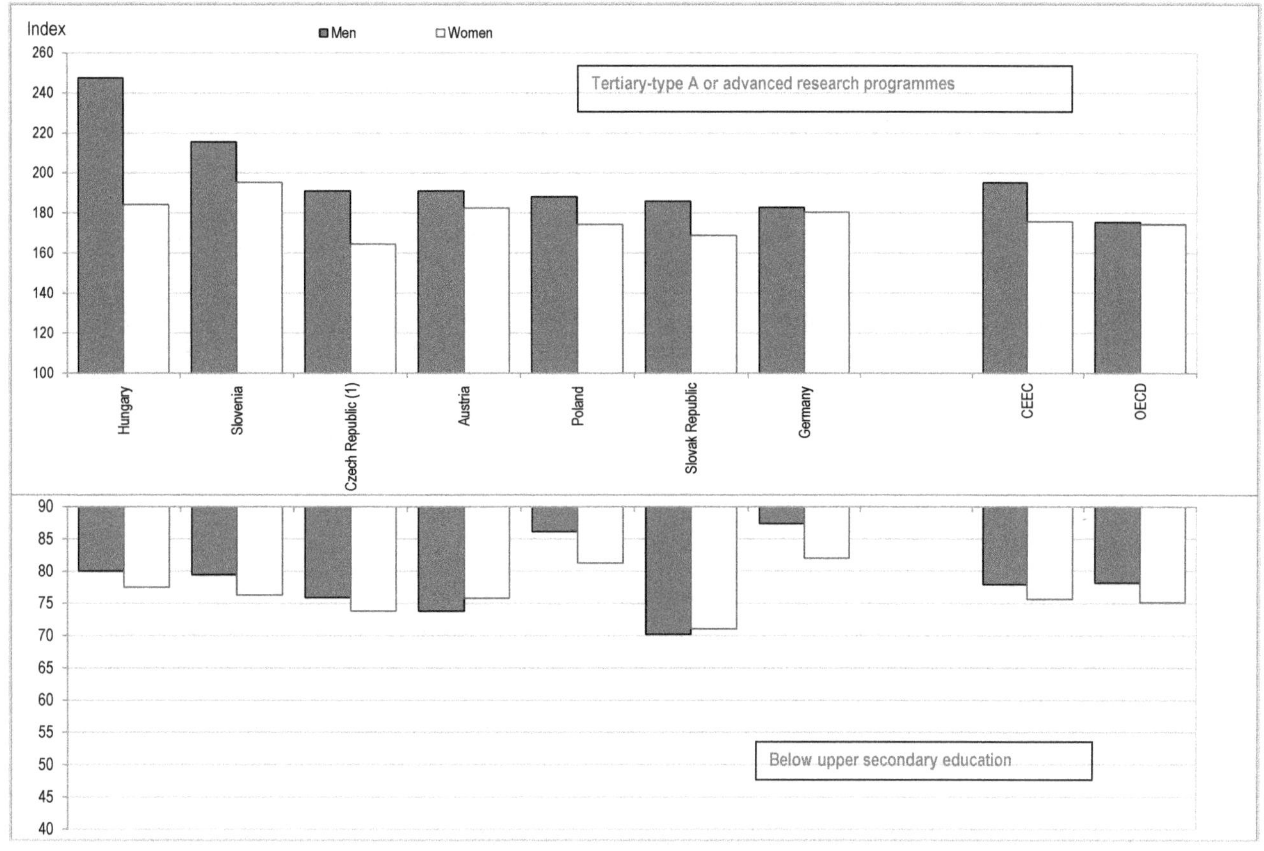

1: Data refer to 2011 rather than 2012.

Source: OECD (2014), *Education at a Glance 2014: OECD Indicators*, OECD Publishing, Paris, http://dx.doi.org/10.1787/eag-2014-en.

StatLink *http://dx.doi.org/10.1787/888933203244*

Bibliography

European Commission (2012), "The European Higher Education Area in 2012: Bologna Process Implementation", Brussels.

Lisko, Ilona (2009), "Vocational Training and Early School Leavers", in *Green Book for the Renewal of Education in Hungary*, Ecostat Government Institute for Strategic Research of Economy and Society, Budapest.

OECD (2014), *Education at a Glance 2014: OECD Indicators*, OECD Publishing, Paris, http://dx.doi.org/10.1787/eag-2014-en.

OECD (2013a), "PISA: Programme for International Student Assessment", *OECD Education Statistics* (database), http://dx.doi.org/10.1787/data-00365-en (accessed on 21 March 2015).

OECD (2013b), *PISA 2012 Results: Excellence through Equity (Volume II): Giving Every Student the Chance to Succeed*, PISA, OECD Publishing, Paris, http://dx.doi.org/10.1787/9789264201132-en.

OECD (2012), *Equity and Quality in Education: Supporting Disadvantaged Students and Schools*, OECD Publishing, Paris, http://dx.doi.org/10.1787/9789264130852-en.

Varga, Julia (2013), "Labour Market Success of Hungarian Higher Education Graduates in 2011", in *Hungarian Graduates 2011*, Education Public Services, Ministry for Human Resources, Budapest.

International surveys measuring confidence and satisfaction with government, institutions and services: Weblinks

Gallup World Poll: www.gallup.com.

ANNEX A

Government expenditures by function as a percentage of GDP, 2012

	Total	General public services	Defence	Public order and safety	Econo-mic affairs	Environ-mental protection	Housing and community amenities	Health	Recrea-tion, culture and religion	Educa-tion	Social protection
Austria	51.7	6.7	0.7	1.5	5.8	0.5	0.6	7.9	1.0	5.6	21.4
Czech Republic	44.5	5.0	0.9	1.8	5.6	1.4	0.7	7.8	2.7	4.8	13.8
Germany	44.7	6.1	1.1	1.6	3.4	0.6	0.5	7.0	0.8	4.3	19.4
Hungary	48.7	9.0	0.8	2.0	6.2	0.7	0.9	5.3	1.9	4.8	17.1
Poland	42.3	6.0	1.2	1.7	4.7	0.6	0.8	4.6	1.2	5.5	16.1
Slovak Republic	37.8	6.0	1.0	2.4	3.5	0.9	0.8	6.2	1.0	3.9	12.1
Slovenia	48.1	5.8	1.1	1.8	3.9	0.7	0.8	7.0	1.8	6.4	18.9
CEEC	43.1	5.7	1.1	1.9	4.4	0.9	0.8	6.4	1.7	5.1	15.2
OECD	45.8	6.5	1.5	1.7	4.4	0.7	0.7	6.7	1.3	5.6	16.7

Note: For "OECD" data, Canada, Chile, Mexico and New Zealand are not included. Data for Australia, Korea and Turkey refer to 2011, rather than 2012. Data for Australia are based on Government Finance Statistics provided by the Australian Bureau of Statistics.

Source: OECD (2014), *OECD National Accounts Statistics* (database), http://dx.doi.org/10.1787/na-data-en (accessed on 21 March 2015).

StatLink http://dx.doi.org/10.1787/888933203330

ANNEX B

Classification of the Functions of Government (COFOG)

Developed by the OECD, the Classification of the Functions of Government (COFOG) classifies government expenditure data from the *System of National Accounts* by the purpose for which the funds are used. As Table B.1 illustrates, first-level COFOG splits expenditure data into ten "functional" groups or sub-sectors of expenditures (such as defence, education and social protection), and second-level COFOG further splits each first-level group into up to nine sub-groups. While first-level COFOG data are available for 32 out of the 34 OECD countries, second-level COFOG data are currently only available for 21 OECD European Union member countries, plus Japan.[1]

Table B.1. **First- and second-level COFOG**

First-level	Second-level
General public services	Executive and legislative organs, financial and fiscal affairs, external affairs Foreign economic aid General services Basic research R&D general public services General public services n.e.c. Public debt transactions Transfers of a general character between different levels of government
Defence	Military defence Civil defence Foreign military aid R&D defence Defence n.e.c.
Public order and safety	Police services Fire-protection services Law courts Prisons R&D public order and safety Public order and safety n.e.c.
Economic affairs	General economic, commercial and labour affairs Agriculture, forestry, fishing and hunting Fuel and energy Mining, manufacturing and construction Transport Communication Other industries R&D economic affairs Economic affairs n.e.c.

Table B.1. **First- and second-level COFOG** *(cont.)*

First-level	Second-level
Environmental protection	Waste management
	Waste water management
	Pollution abatement
	Protection of biodiversity and landscape
	R&D environmental protection
	Environmental protection n.e.c.
Housing and community amenities	Housing development
	Community development
	Water supply
	Street lighting
	R&D housing and community amenities
	Housing and community amenities n.e.c.
Health	Medical products, appliances and equipment
	Outpatient services
	Hospital services
	Public health services
	R&D health
	Health n.e.c.
Recreation, culture and religion	Recreational and sporting services
	Cultural services
	Broadcasting and publishing services
	Religious and other community services
	R&D recreation, culture and religion
	Recreation, culture and religion n.e.c.
Education	Pre-primary and primary education
	Secondary education
	Post-secondary non-tertiary education
	Tertiary education
	Education not definable by level
	Subsidiary services to education
	R&D education
	Education n.e.c.
Social protection	Sickness and disability
	Old age
	Survivors
	Family and children
	Unemployment
	Housing
	Social exclusion n.e.c.
	R&D social protection
	Social protection n.e.c

Note: n.e.c.: "not elsewhere classified".

Notes

1. First-level COFOG data are not available for Chile and Mexico. Until recently, second level COFOG data were available in some national statistical offices, but were not collected by international organisations. Moreover, the second-level COFOG data were not comparable among countries because the SNA/UN guide and the International Monetary Fund Manual on Government Finance Statistics do not provide much practical information on the application of COFOG concepts. However, in 2005, Eurostat established a task force to develop a manual on the application of COFOG to national account expenditure data and to discuss the collection of second-level COFOG data for European countries. Second-level COFOG data are not available for Switzerland and all non-European member countries of the OECD (except Japan): Australia, Canada, Chile, Israel, Korea, Mexico, New Zealand and the United States. In addition, these data are available only for selected COFOG divisions in some members of the European Union. Efforts are underway to reach agreement with these countries about the submission of these data to the OECD.

ANNEX C

Political system in Hungary

Population mid-2011 estimate (in millions)	9 971 726
Member of the European Union	Yes
State structure	Unitary
Number of tiers of government	
State/regional	20
Provincial	Not applicable
Local	3 176
System of executive power	Parliamentary
Head of state	President
Head of government	Prime Minister
Existence of term limits for presidents	
Is there a president?	Yes
Term limit (years)	10
Governments at the central level between 1992 and 2012	
Total number of governments	10
Number of coalition governments	7
Number of executives serving non-consecutive terms	8
Number of ministers at the central level of government (2013)	8
Number of ministries or departments at the central level of government (2013)	8
Upper House (central government)	
Existence	No
Membership based on regional considerations?	Not applicable
Frequency of elections (in years)	Not applicable
Size – number of seats	Not applicable
Lower House (central government)	
Electoral system	Multi Member - Proportional
Frequency of elections (in years)	4
Size – number of seats	199
Existence of system of judicial review of the constitutionality of laws and actions	Judicial review

ANNEX D

Economic context in Hungary

Macroeconomic indicators and projections change, volume (2005 prices) | Annual percentage

	2010 current prices (billion HUF)	2011	2012	2013	2014	2015
GDP	**26513**	**1.6**	**-1.7**	**1.2**	**2.0**	**1.6**
Private consumption	14074	0.4	-1.6	0.2	1.6	1.1
Government consumption	5827	0.0	-1.2	1.6	1.0	-0.1
Gross fixed capital formation	4920	-5.9	-3.7	5.9	3.1	1.5
Housing [1]	659	-27.4	-11.8	-9.2	-2.6	-0.9
Final domestic demand	24821	-1.0	-1.9	1.6	1.8	0.9
Stockbuilding [1 2]	190	0.4	-1.5	1.0	0.2	0.0
Total domestic demand	25012	-0.5	-3.5	0.8	1.5	0.9
Exports of goods and services	22552	8.4	1.7	5.3	5.3	5.4
Imports of goods and services	21050	6.4	-0.1	5.3	4.6	5.0
Net exports [1 2]	1502	2.1	1.6	-0.3	1.0	0.8
Other indicators (growth rates, unless specified)						
Potential GDP		0.2	0.1	0.3	0.6	1.1
Output gap[3]		-1.5	-3.3	-2.6	-1.5	-1.0
Employment		0.8	1.7	1.6	2.6	-0.1
Unemployment rate		10.9	11.0	10.2	8.7	8.9
GDP deflator		2.6	3.0	3.0	2.3	2.7
Consumer price index (headline inflation)		3.9	5.7	1.7	0.5	2.8
Core consumer prices		1.0	3.9	3.8	2.9	3.0
Household saving ratio, net[4]		5.4	1.9	4.0	5.4	5.1
Current account balance [5]		0.4	0.8	3.0	3.6	3.9
General government financial balance[5]		4.2	-2.2	-2.3	-2.9	-2.9
Underlying general government financial balance[3]		-4.2	-1.6	-1.5	-2.8	-2.6
Underlying general government primary balance[3]		-0.5	2.3	2.4	1.2	1.4
Gross government debt (Maastricht)[5]		81.8	79.7	78.8	79.7	79.5
General government net debt[5]		53.1	61.1	62.8	63.1	63.4
Three-month money market rate, average		6.0	6.9	4.2	2.9	3.3
Ten-year government bond yield, average		7.6	7.9	5.9	5.5	5.4

1. OECD (2013), "OECD Economic Outlook No. 94", *OECD Economic Outlook: Statistics and Projections* (database), http://dx.doi.org/10.1787/data-00676-en (accessed on 21 March 2015).

2. Contribution to changes in real GDP.

3. As a percentage of potential GDP.

4. As a percentage of household disposable income.

5. As a percentage of GDP.

Source: OECD (2014), "OECD Economic Outlook No. 95", *OECD Economic Outlook: Statistics and Projections* (database), http://dx.doi.org/10.1787/data-00688-en (accessed on 21 March 2015); OECD (2013), "OECD Economic Outlook No. 94", *OECD Economic Outlook: Statistics and Projections* (database), http://dx.doi.org/10.1787/data-00676-en (accessed on 21 March 2015).

ANNEX E

The tree structure of the new Product Market Regulation (PMR) indicator set

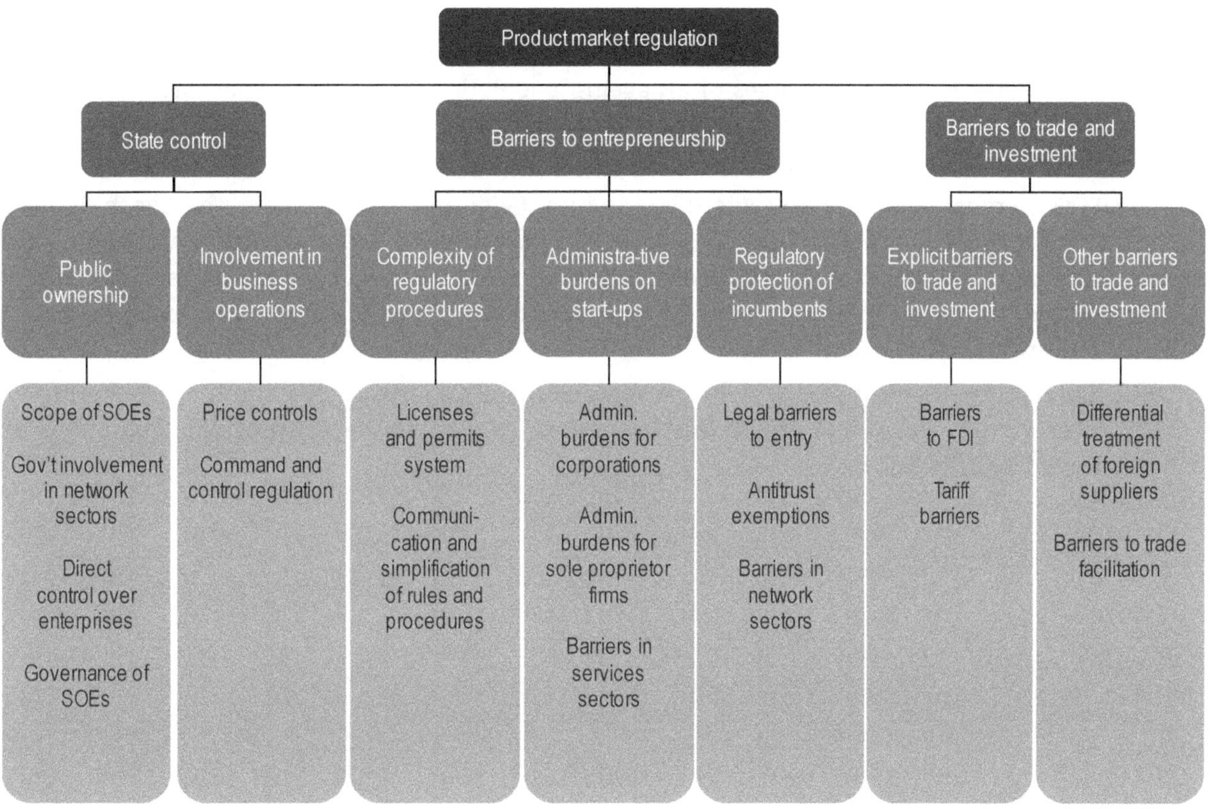

Note: Additional details regarding the theoretical framework, construction and country scores of each composite are available at www.oecd.org/economy/growth/indicatorsofproductmarketregulationhomepage.html.

ORGANISATION FOR ECONOMIC CO-OPERATION AND DEVELOPMENT

The OECD is a unique forum where governments work together to address the economic, social and environmental challenges of globalisation. The OECD is also at the forefront of efforts to understand and to help governments respond to new developments and concerns, such as corporate governance, the information economy and the challenges of an ageing population. The Organisation provides a setting where governments can compare policy experiences, seek answers to common problems, identify good practice and work to co-ordinate domestic and international policies.

The OECD member countries are: Australia, Austria, Belgium, Canada, Chile, the Czech Republic, Denmark, Estonia, Finland, France, Germany, Greece, Hungary, Iceland, Ireland, Israel, Italy, Japan, Korea, Luxembourg, Mexico, the Netherlands, New Zealand, Norway, Poland, Portugal, the Slovak Republic, Slovenia, Spain, Sweden, Switzerland, Turkey, the United Kingdom and the United States. The European Commission takes part in the work of the OECD.

OECD Publishing disseminates widely the results of the Organisation's statistics gathering and research on economic, social and environmental issues, as well as the conventions, guidelines and standards agreed by its members.

OECD PUBLISHING, 2, rue André-Pascal, 75775 PARIS CEDEX 16
(42 2015 09 1 P) ISBN 978-92-64-23352-2 – 2015-17

www.ingramcontent.com/pod-product-compliance
Lightning Source LLC
LaVergne TN
LVHW081413110826
845149LV00010B/1731